INT   RADE:

book

About Island Press

Island Press is the only nonprofit organization in the United States whose principal purpose is the publication of books on environmental issues and natural resource management. We provide solutions-oriented information to professionals, public officials, business and community leaders, and concerned citizens who are shaping responses to environmental problems.

In 1994, Island Press celebrates its tenth anniversary as the leading provider of timely and practical books that take a multidisciplinary approach to critical environmental concerns. Our growing list of titles reflects our commitment to bringing the best of an expanding body of literature to the environmental community throughout North America and the world.

Support for Island Press is provided by The Geraldine R. Dodge Foundation, The Energy Foundation, The Ford Foundation, The George Gund Foundation, William and Flora Hewlett Foundation, The James Irvine Foundation, The John D. and Catherine T. MacArthur Foundation, The Andrew W. Mellon Foundation, The Joyce Mertz-Gilmore Foundation, The New-Land Foundation, The Pew Charitable Trusts, The Rockefeller Brothers Fund, The Tides Foundation, Turner Foundation, Inc., The Rockefeller Philanthropic Collaborative, Inc., and individual donors.

About World Wildlife Fund

World Wildlife Fund (WWF) is the largest private U.S. conservation organization that works worldwide to conserve nature. WWF programs aim to preserve the diversity and abundance of life on Earth and the health of ecological systems by protecting natural areas and wildlife populations, promoting sustainable use of natural resources, and promoting more efficient resource and energy use and the maximum reduction of pollution. WWF is affiliated with the international WWF network, which has national organizations, associates, or representatives in nearly 40 countries. In the United States, WWF has more than 1 million members.

INTERNATIONAL WILDLIFE TRADE:
A CITES Sourcebook

Ginette Hemley, Editor

World Wildlife Fund
Washington, D.C.

WWF

ISLAND PRESS
Washington, D.C.
Covelo, California

Design by Panache Design

ISBN 1-55963-348-4

Library of Congress Cataloging-in-Publication Data

International wildlife trade: a CITES sourcebook/ Ginette Hemley, editor,
    p.   cm.
    Includes bibliographical references and index.
    ISBN 1-55963-348-4 (acid-free paper)
    1. Endangered species—Law and legislation. 2. Wild animal trade—Law and legislation. 3. Convention on International Trade in Endangered Species of Wild Fauna and Flora (1973) I. Hemley, Ginette. II. Convention on International Trade in Endangered Species of Wild Fauna and Flora (1973)
K3525.I58   1994
341.7'625—dc20   94-32179
                                                          CIP

Printed on recycled, acid-free paper, using soy-based inks.

Manufactured in the United States of America

10 9 8 7 6 5 4 3 2 1

Contents

Foreword

Twenty years of worldwide efforts to enforce laws governing trade in endangered wildlife have yielded predictably mixed results. On the one hand, the rule of law and the threat of trade sanctions often seem powerless to halt trade in species like tigers and rhinos, even though these species are on the brink of extinction. On the other hand, the international ivory ban and measures to control and regulate trade in spotted cats and crocodiles have produced encouraging results. So it is that the November 1994 conference of the Parties to the Convention on International Trade in Endangered Species of Wild Fauna and Flora (CITES) illustrates how far we have come in 20 years—and how far we have yet to go.

CITES is in many ways the benchmark international conservation agreement because more than 120 nations are pledged to implement its provisions. Five years ago, CITES Parties added the African elephant to Appendix I, thereby prohibiting its international trade. Although hotly contested at the time, this listing, coupled with increased investments in field-based conservation projects, is credited with breaking the back of the massive illegal ivory trade and beginning to stabilize African elephant populations.

Although the elephant conservation challenge goes far beyond illegal commerce in ivory, there is little doubt that wildlife trade is big business. A conservative estimate places the value worldwide at more than $10 billion a year with at least $2–3 billion of that illegal. If uncontrolled, even legal wildlife trade can have devastating effects. Developing countries, which provide most of the wild animals and plants in trade, earn foreign exchange from this trade and local populations earn their living from it. If, however, the level of trade exceeds the natural ability of wildlife populations to replenish themselves, the income from wildlife trade will disappear along with the species.

Illegal wildlife trade is pushing to the brink of extinction species like rhinos and tigers. Even though they are listed in Appendix I of CITES, fewer than 11,000 rhinos and 6,000 tigers remain in the wild. Should either or both species become extinct, the treaty's effectiveness will surely be called into question. CITES will not last another 20 years unless enforcement mechanisms are strengthened and the community of nations that are parties to the convention join forces to uphold its provisions.

With the issues facing CITES and wildlife conservation in general becoming more complex each day, we have prepared this CITES Sourcebook to give the treaty parties and all conservationists information about the treaty, specific wildlife trade issues, the role of wildlife trade in conservation, and the significance of this trade at local, national, and international levels.

Kathryn S. Fuller
President, World Wildlife Fund-U.S.

Introduction

For more than two decades, the Convention on International Trade in Endangered Species of Wild Fauna and Flora, known as CITES, has been the largest and, by some accounts, the most effective international wildlife conservation agreement in the world. CITES acts as the ultimate traffic cop, deciding when international trade in certain species, whether the African elephant, jaguar, or exotic birds, can continue unimpeded, when it must slow, and when it must stop entirely to avoid the tragedy of extinction.

When the treaty was signed in Washington, D.C., on March 3, 1973, the Parties were concerned primarily with the effects of rampaging trade on a few well-known species such as spotted cats, chimpanzees, and crocodiles. Today the context has changed because the maturing sciences of ecology and conservation biology have given us a deeper understanding of how ecosystems function. This understanding makes it clear that uncontrolled trade and eventual loss of a wide range of species can have consequences far more disturbing than could have been imagined in 1973.

In the grand scheme of environmental hazards, the demise of the Mariana fruit bat may seem a relative trifle, but this little-known species from the South Pacific is a case in point. In search of fruit, flowers, and nectar, the bat flies from plant to plant. As it makes its rounds, the bat carries pollen from one plant to another. Many plants on the Mariana islands and elsewhere in the South Pacific have evolved together with the fruit bat to the point that these plants rely entirely on fruit bats for pollination.

Fruit bats in the South Pacific face severe threats stemming from international wildlife trade as well as the loss of habitat to development. For millennia, fruit bats have been a popular delicacy on the island of Guam, particularly among Guam's indigenous people, the Chamorros. Since World War II, as ancient hunting methods have been replaced by firearms, bat populations have been nearly wiped out. The Pacific islands now export thousands of bat carcasses annually to Guam.

If the bats disappear, the plants dependent on them as pollinators may vanish as well. This, in turn, could mark the beginning of a process that sends extinction cascading along the food chain, leading to severely impaired ecosystems and a collapse of the region's biological diversity.

The conservation of biological diversity is a relatively new role for CITES, which provides the mechanisms for controlling the trade in fruit bats and other ecologically and commercially important species. Since its inception, CITES has been viewed almost exclusively as a "species" mechanism without broader ecological concerns. It is in the broad context, however, where CITES may make its greatest contribution.

An examination of the species most threatened by trade reveals that many, like the Mariana fruit bat, fill important ecological niches. Elephants and rhinos, for example, help to reshape the environment by knocking over trees and clearing grasslands. Macaws form a crucial link in tropical forest ecosystems by dispersing plant seeds throughout the forest. Because they keep populations of prey species in check, large predators like bears and tigers are key links in the food chain. Corals build reefs that shelter an astounding diversity of marine life, protect the young of commercially valuable marine food species, and serve as natural barriers against beach and island erosion. Because these and other species form vital linkages in the complex web of life on Earth, it is important to ensure that international wildlife trade does not threaten their existence.

A particularly challenging and complex aspect of that trade is the huge and lucrative market for oriental medicines. Demand for these medicines provides the financial incentive for poachers to hunt some of the most endangered species on Earth. Horns of rhinoceros and saiga antelope, bones of tigers and leopards, musk pods from musk deer glands, bile salts from bear gallbladders, and penises from northern fur seals and tigers are just some examples of species parts and products used in oriental medicines. The increasing affluence of Asians; the growth of immigrant Asian communities in Europe and North America; the new-found interest of both Asians and non-Asians in self-healing and herbal medicines, including traditional oriental medicines; and the overall growth in international trade in the last half of the twentieth century have all contributed to increased trade in oriental medicines. Many wildlife populations, already under pressure from habitat loss, cannot sustain this increased demand.

Like the trade in fruit bats in the South Pacific, the oriental medicinal trade has ancient ties to indigenous culture. Any effort to curb it and prevent the use of endangered species must include comprehensive public awareness campaigns to reduce demand among Asian and non-Asian consumers and promote the use of substitutes. Enforcement of international wildlife laws, especially CITES regulations, also will be crucial.

The difficulties of controlling a market as complex and deeply rooted as the oriental medicinal trade reveals both the strengths and weaknesses of CITES as it now stands. The treaty's strength lies in the basic principle of strictly limiting international trade in species in genuine need of protection while allowing controlled trade in species that are capable of sustaining some level of exploitation. Species such as tigers and rhinos clearly cannot survive in the face of large-scale trade to supply medicinal markets. Yet, certain crocodilians, tegu lizards, and other species remain plentiful despite steady global demand for their products because management schemes and export controls have been relatively effective.

The treaty's weaknesses lie in its implementation and enforcement mechanisms. Each member state is responsible for enforcing CITES decisions, although the ability and commitment to enforce these decisions varies widely among countries. The CITES Secretariat in Switzerland, whose function is to oversee the trade control system at the international level, has limited enforcement authority. Yet CITES has created quota systems for certain species that cannot function without some sort of centralized monitoring capability. Even unilateral quotas, such as the recently imposed U.S. limit on the number of parrots imported into the country, can be difficult to manage.

A major obstacle to strengthening the international enforcement of CITES is the relationship of wildlife trade to broader international commerce. CITES highlights a fundamental trade and environment issue: Can international trade law distinguish between one product that is produced in a sustainable fashion and another that is not? The question will become more and more critical as governments and international donors search for ways to use natural resources without destroying the productive capacity of ecosystems. The major trade agreements, the General Agreement on Tariffs and Trade (GATT), and the North American Free Trade Agreement (NAFTA) do not allow such a distinction. Under both GATT and NAFTA, for example, a crocodile skin briefcase made from farm-raised animals is equivalent to one made from wild animals.

CITES has the potential of bringing the idea of sustainability into international trade law for the first time. As it now stands, CITES allows limited trade in those species that might face extinction if trade continued unchecked. Those species can be traded under certain circumstances, depending on the biological status of the species and the degree to which they are affected by trade. Adding the question of whether the exploitation of these species is sustainable as a further criteria would mark a significant step toward bringing this vital issue into the international debate over trade and the environment. It is in this context that the relationship between CITES and the Convention on Biological Diversity will become increasingly important.

In addition to resolving difficult questions about enforcement, international trade, and funding, CITES Parties must also confront questions that go to the heart of the treaty itself. The treaty includes three lists or "appendices" (pp. 59–118). Appendix I lists species threatened with extinction and essentially prohibits their trade. Appendix II lists species not yet threatened with extinction but likely to become so if trade is not controlled. Appendix III allows a country to list a species already protected within its own borders so as to enlist the help of other CITES members in enforcing national wildlife laws.

Although the three appendices are the foundation of CITES, the treaty itself provides only general guidelines for including species on the lists, moving them from one appendix to another, or removing them should the threat to their survival diminish. It was not until 1976 at a conference in Berne that the member states designed specific criteria. These so-called "Berne criteria" have become the focus of growing controversy because, some argue, they have allowed politics—rather than science—to be the deciding factor in species listing. Advances in conservation biology over the past two decades dictate the need for more objective and scientific criteria for protecting species, while at the same time retaining the crucial "precautionary principle," which specifies that any decrease in protection should be approached with caution and that CITES member states should always err on the side of conservation. Carefully crafted revisions in the Berne criteria should strengthen CITES and help CITES nations to protect better those species that are threatened by trade.

The issues facing CITES, and indeed those facing wildlife conservation in general, become more complex each day. The outcome of the ongoing debates about trade and funding issues, as well as the criteria for listing species, will help determine whether CITES remains a central tool for conserving life on Earth.

—Ginette Hemley

1/How CITES Works

The only global treaty that aims to regulate the trade in threatened and endangered species, the Convention on International Trade in Endangered Species of Wild Fauna and Flora (CITES) was signed in Washington, D.C., on March 3, 1973, and entered into force in July 1975.

According to the treaty's preamble, parties to CITES recognize "that wild fauna and flora in their many beautiful and varied forms are an irreplaceable part of the natural systems of the earth" and that wildlife has many values, including aesthetic, scientific, cultural, recreational, and economic. CITES parties also recognize that "peoples and States are and should be the best protectors of their own wild fauna and flora."

The 21 initial signatory nations were Argentina, Belgium, Brazil, Costa Rica, Cyprus, Denmark, France, West Germany, Guatemala, Iran, Italy, Luxembourg, Mauritius, Panama, Philippines, the Socialist Republic of Vietnam, South Africa, Thailand, the United Kingdom, the United States, and Venezuela. Presently 122 countries are parties to CITES. South Korea, Vietnam, and St. Kitts/Nevis are the most recent countries to join the treaty.

CORE FUNCTIONS

Parties to the CITES treaty are obliged to monitor the global trade in wildlife and wildlife products and take action on behalf of species that may be headed for trouble as a result of international trade. At the heart of the treaty are three Appendices that enumerate species facing some degree of threat. The most restrictive list is Appendix I, which covers species that are threatened with extinction and that are or may be affected by trade. With certain narrow exceptions, all international trade in the roughly 675 Appendix I species is forbidden. Species listed in Appendix II may not be threatened now with extinction but they could become threatened unless their trade is strictly regulated. The more than 25,000 species listed in Appendix II (including some 3,700 animals and more than 21,000 plants) may be traded, provided certain conditions are met that ensure the species will not be harmed by the trade. Appendix III is an optional list that parties may use to protect native species that might be threatened by trade.

CITES also establishes other mechanisms for supporting the global structure for regulating trade in species included in these all-important lists. Full-time staff at the Geneva-based CITES Secretariat monitor treaty implementation and infractions, administer scientific studies for species affected by trade, identify problems or challenges in enforcing CITES decisions, and help organize major CITES meetings. Government agencies and nongovernmental organizations (NGOs) play a key supporting role monitoring trade, gathering field information, analyzing data, and developing new proposals.

The CITES party nations meet every two to two-and-a-half years at the Conference of the Parties (COP) to review how well the convention is working, amend the appendices, and resolve policy issues. COPs have engendered increasing visibility in recent years, as the parties have had to grapple with such controversial decisions as the 1989 Appendix I listing for the African elephant, which banned all international trade in elephant ivory.

SPECIAL COMMITTEES

During the early years of the treaty, a standing committee was created to address issues that arose during intervals between COPs. A technical committee was also set up to deal with specific plant and animal issues relating to CITES. In 1987, the sixth COP adopted a resolution that created formal Animals and Plants Committees, abolished the Technical Committee, and reestablished the Standing Committee.

The *Standing Committee* provides general policy and operational direction to the Secretariat concerning implementation and enforcement of the convention. The committee gives advice on the preparation of meeting agendas and other requirements, reviews major country infraction problems, carries out interim activities on behalf of the conference, and drafts resolutions for COP consideration. Members of the Standing Committee are elected from the six major geographic regions after every other COP. The Standing Committee normally meets twice each year. The meetings are closed to the public.

The Standing Committee has been the source of growing attention and controversy as it faces pressure to respond to serious enforcement and implementation problems. Recent concerns about the severe endangerment of rhinos and tigers through illegal trade in their parts led to a series of Standing Committee decisions citing certain countries for their continued failure to curtail this trade within their borders. Some party nations have argued that the Standing Committee has exceeded its authority in seeking to enforce the treaty, while other parties maintain that the Standing Committee has been too weak and too diffident and that this role of a senior committee is essential to the effective administration of the treaty.

The *Animals Committee* reviews technical issues associated with trade in CITES-listed animal species, assists in the development and maintenance of a standardized animal names list, monitors the status and trade of animals on Appendix II (see page 85) that are considered to be significantly affected by trade, reviews the trade of Appendix II-listed species to determine whether trade is still a threat to their survival, and drafts resolutions on animal matters for consideration by the COP. The Animals Committee reports to the Standing Committee and the COP. It generally meets once a year and is open to approved observers who wish to attend.

The *Plants Committee* has the same responsibilities with respect to CITES-listed plants as the Animals Committee has for animals.

The Standing Committee and Animals and Plants Committees sometimes establish formal working groups to address complex issues requiring special attention, such as the transport needs and treatment of live animals in trade.

TREATY APPENDICES

CITES categorizes plant and animal species in three lists or "appendices." Inclusion in these appendices obligates parties to institute specific import and/or export controls on listed species.

Appendix I lists species that are threatened with extinction and are or may be affected by international trade. Included in this appendix are all rhinos, sea turtles, great apes, great whales, most large cats, and some 600 other endangered species. CITES generally bans commercial trade in Appendix I-listed species and allows noncommercial trade in them only in exceptional circumstance, such as for scientific or zoological purposes, if such trade will not jeopardize their chances for survival.

All international transactions in Appendix I-listed species require an export permit from the country where the wildlife originates or a reexport certificate from the reexporting country and an import permit from the recipient country. To ensure that both trading parties are aware of and agree to the rules governing the transaction, the import permit must be issued *before* the export permit can be issued.

Appendix II regulates commerce in wildlife that is not already threatened with extinction but may become so if trade is not controlled. The convention permits commercial trade in species listed in Appendix II, provided that the country of origin or country of reexport has issued an export permit or reexport certificate.

The appendices include look-alike species that are not threatened themselves but closely resemble other listed species. An entire genus, family, or order might also be listed if most species in the group are threatened and if it is difficult to distinguish between threatened and nonthreatened species. For example, Appendix II covers all parrots, cats, crocodilians, boids, orchids, and cacti not already listed in Appendix I. This helps customs officials recognize that any shipment containing these look-alike groups should be checked.

Appendix III gives parties the option of listing native species that are already protected within their own borders. This measure is intended to help CITES parties gain other nations' cooperation in enforcing their own wildlife trade regulations. Canada, for example, lists the walrus in Appendix III because the government regulates trade in the species and wants other countries to regulate imports of walrus from Canada.

OBLIGATIONS OF CITES PARTIES

When a country becomes a party to CITES, it agrees to fulfill certain obligations described in the treaty text. It must set up management and scientific authorities independent of each other to assess and regulate trade and to issue the necessary CITES permits; submit annual reports on all CITES trade; participate in the COPs reviewing implementation, enforcement, and policies of CITES; and amend treaty appendices as necessary. As is the case with most other international agreements, CITES leaves it up to individual countries to decide how best they might fulfill these responsibilities.

Enforcement

Because CITES can only be enforced by its individual members, the treaty's success depends on the national and political will of each party. In many countries, customs officials or, in a few countries, wildlife inspectors are in charge of inspecting shipments and seizing contraband. Special wildlife agents investigate illegal trade schemes in many countries. The CITES parties are committed to confiscation of smuggled or contraband goods and to return these back to the country of origin, when possible and appropriate. Parties are also obliged to penalize violators and must establish fines and other penalties as appropriate.

National Legislation to Implement CITES

After a country joins CITES, it should be prepared to take appropriate, usually legislative, measures to implement the convention, although the treaty does not specifically require legislation. At a minimum, the legislation should commit the country to abide by all CITES mandates, and it may also incorporate measures stricter than the convention itself. Unfortunately, many countries who have been members for years have not taken these steps.

The United States implements CITES through the U.S. Endangered Species Act (ESA). CITES controls prescribed by the act prohibit the import, export, or reexport of Appendix I, II, or III species without the required permits and also forbid the trade or possession of any species imported, exported, or reexported into or from the United States in contravention of the convention. Those who knowingly violate CITES, whether for personal or commercial reasons, may have their goods confiscated and receive penalties of up to one year in jail and as much as $100,000 in fines per violation ($200,000 for organizations). Under the ESA, the Secretary of the Interior is designated to implement CITES in the United States. Most of this responsibility has been delegated to the U.S. Fish and Wildlife Service.

Management and Scientific Authorities

CITES parties are required to set up one or more management authorities to regulate trade and one or more scientific authorities to deliberate on scientific issues related to the trade and exploitation of species for commerce. The management authority issues import and export permits and certificates and compiles information on annual trade. The scientific authority determines whether particular trade will be detrimental to the survival of the species involved and whether captive conditions are suitable for live animals in trade. The scientific authority monitors export volumes and their impact on protected native species and oversees other CITES scientific matters. The scientific authority often reviews permit applications and proposed changes to the CITES appendices.

Management authority responsibilities are usually undertaken by a government office. In the United States, the designated office is the Office of Management Authority of the Fish and Wildlife Service in the Department of the Interior. The scientific authority is often a mixture of experts from the government, academia, zoos, and other institutions. The United States has established the Office of the Scientific Authority in the Fish and Wildlife Service.

Finances

CITES is financed primarily by contributions from member countries. Each party's requested annual payment is based on the United Nations contribution scale. Requested payments range from $300 or so for the smaller, poorer members to more than $1 million for the wealthiest. (The U.S. contribution, at about 25 percent of CITES' budget, is the highest on the scale.) These contributions support the CITES Secretariat and activities that help countries regulate their wildlife resources. In recent years, CITES funds have partially financed training seminars for officials from Latin America, Africa, and Asia. Some studies and seminars are funded by conservation NGOs like World Wildlife Fund or by trade or industry groups.

As with other international programs financed by voluntary contributions, CITES is continually short of funds. In recent years, as many as one-third of the parties have not paid their annual share.

THE ROLE OF NONGOVERNMENTAL ORGANIZATIONS

CITES is unique in that it specifically allows for the active participation of NGOs in many treaty activities. NGOs are a crucial force in promoting strong implementation of CITES. Traditionally, NGOs representing conservationists, wildlife and industry interests, and the scientific community have been active participants in the biennial COP, although they are not allowed to vote. NGOs are allowed, by approval of their country of residence or by the chairman of the CITES committees, to participate in the COP and in the Animals and Plants Committees meetings and special working groups.

6

NGOs sometimes make important financial contributions to CITES activities. They occasionally pay travel expenses for conference delegates from developing countries; contribute to the Secretariat's work; provide funds for scientific studies of CITES species; and help finance and organize training seminars for wildlife trade enforcement officers.

Some NGOs also provide technical support to trade officials and carry out public awareness campaigns to end illegal wildlife trade. The NGOs' most important contributions may be as watchdogs: Some conservation NGOs alert government officials to potential infractions, investigate illicit trade routes and operations, and pressure authorities in importing and exporting countries to improve their laws and enforcement efforts.

CONVENTION ON INTERNATIONAL TRADE IN ENDANGERED SPECIES OF WILD FAUNA AND FLORA (CITES)

Signed at Washington, D.C., March 3, 1973

The Contracting States,

Recognizing that wild fauna and flora in their many beautiful and varied forms are an irreplaceable part of the natural systems of the earth which must be protected for this and the generations to come;

Conscious of the ever-growing value of wild fauna and flora from aesthetic, scientific, cultural, recreational and economic points of view;

Recognizing that peoples and States are and should be the best protectors of their own wild fauna and flora;

Recognizing, in addition, that international cooperation is essential for the protection of certain species of wild fauna and flora against over-exploitation through international trade;

Convinced of the urgency of taking appropriate measures to this end;

Have agreed as follows:

Article I

Definitions
For the purpose of the present Convention, unless the context otherwise requires:
  (a) "Species" means any species, subspecies or geographically separate population thereof;

(b) "Specimen" means:
  (i) any animal or plant, whether alive or dead;
  (ii) in the case of an animal: for species included in Appendices I and II, any readily recognizable part or derivative thereof; and for species included in Appendix III, any readily recognizable part or derivative thereof specified in Appendix III in relation to the species; and
  (iii) in the case of a plant: for species included in Appendix I, any readily recognizable part or derivative thereof; and for species included in Appendices II and III, any readily recognizable part or derivative thereof specified in Appendices II and III in relation to the species;
(c) "Trade" means export, re-export, import and introduction from the sea;
(d) "Re-export" means export of any specimen that has previously been imported;
(e) "Introduction from the sea" means transportation into a State of specimens of any species which were taken in the marine environment not under the jurisdiction of any State;
(f) "Scientific Authority" means a national scientific authority designated in accordance with Article IX;
(g) "Management Authority" means a national management authority designated in accordance with Article IX;
(h) "Party" means a State for which the present Convention has entered into force.

Article II

Fundamental Principles
1. Appendix I shall include all species threatened with extinction which are or may be affected by trade. Trade in specimens of these species must be subject to particularly strict regulation in order not to endanger further their survival and must only be authorized in exceptional circumstances.
2. Appendix II shall include:
  (a) all species which although not necessarily now threatened with extinction may become so unless trade in specimens of such species is subject to strict regulation in order to avoid utilization incompatible with their survival; and
  (b) other species which must be subject to regulation in order that trade in specimens of certain species referred to in sub-paragraph (a) of this paragraph may be brought under effective control.
3. Appendix III shall include all species which any Party identified as being subject to regulation within its jurisdiction for the purpose of preventing or

restricting exploitation, and as needing the cooperation of other parties in the control of trade.

4. The Parties shall not allow trade in specimens of species included in Appendices I, II and III except in accordance with the provisions of the present Convention.

Article III

Regulation of Trade in Specimens of Species Included in Appendix I

1. All trade in specimens of species included in Appendix I shall be in accordance with the provisions of this Article.

2. The export of any specimen of a species included in Appendix I shall require the prior grant and presentation of an export permit. An export permit shall only be granted when the following conditions have been met:

   (a) a Scientific Authority of the State of export has advised that such export will not be detrimental to the survival of that species;

   (b) a Management Authority of the State of export is satisfied that the specimen was not obtained in contravention of the laws of that State for the protection of fauna and flora;

   (c) a Management Authority of the State of export is satisfied that any living specimen will be so prepared and shipped as to minimize the risk of injury, damage to health or cruel treatment; and

   (d) a Management Authority of the State of export is satisfied that an import permit has been granted for the specimen.

3. The import of any specimen of a species included in Appendix I shall require the prior grant and presentation of an import permit and either an export permit or a re-export certificate. An import permit shall only be granted when the following conditions have been met:

   (a) a Scientific Authority of the State of import has advised that the import will be for purposes which are not detrimental to the survival of the species involved;

   (b) a Scientific Authority of the State of import is satisfied that the proposed recipient of a living specimen is suitably equipped to house and care for it; and

   (c) a Management Authority of the State of import is satisfied that the specimen is not to be used for primarily commercial purposes.

4. The re-export of any specimen of a species included in Appendix I shall require the prior grant and presentation of a re-export certificate. A re-export certificate shall only be granted when the following conditions

have been met:

(a) a Management Authority of the State of re-export is satisfied that the specimen was imported into that State in accordance with the provisions of the present Convention;

(b) a Management Authority of the State of re-export is satisfied that any living specimen will be so prepared and shipped as to minimize the risk of injury, damage to health or cruel treatment; and

(c) a Management Authority of the State of re-export is satisfied that an import permit has been granted for any living specimen.

5. The introduction from the sea of any specimen of a species included in Appendix I shall require the prior grant of a certificate from a Management Authority of the State of introduction. A certificate shall only be granted when the following conditions have been met:

(a) a Scientific Authority of the State of introduction advises that the introduction will not be detrimental to the survival of the species involved;

(b) a Management Authority of the State of introduction is satisfied that the proposed recipient of a living specimen is suitably equipped to house and care for it; and

(c) a Management Authority of the State of introduction is satisfied that the specimen is not to be used for primarily commercial purposes.

Article IV

Regulation of Trade in Specimens of Species Included in Appendix II

1. All trade in specimens of species included in Appendix II shall be in accordance with the provisions of this Article.

2. The export of any specimen of a species included in Appendix II shall require the prior grant and presentation of an export permit. An export permit shall only be granted when the following conditions have been met:

(a) a Scientific Authority of the State of export has advised that such export will not be detrimental to the survival of that species;

(b) a Management Authority of the State of export is satisfied that the specimen was not obtained in contravention of the laws of that State for the protection of fauna and flora; and

(c) a Management Authority of the State of export is satisfied that any living specimen will be so prepared and shipped as to minimize the risk of injury, damage to health or cruel treatment.

3. A Scientific Authority in each Party shall monitor both the export permits

granted by that State for specimens of species included in Appendix II and the actual exports of such specimens. Whenever a Scientific Authority determines that the export of specimens of any such species should be limited in order to maintain that species throughout its range at a level consistent with its role in the ecosystems in which it occurs and well above the level at which that species might become eligible for inclusion in Appendix I, the Scientific Authority shall advise the appropriate Management Authority of suitable measures to be taken to limit the grant of export permits for specimens of that species.

4. The import of any specimen of a species included in Appendix II shall require the prior presentation of either an export permit or a re-export certificate.

5. The re-export of any specimen of a species included in Appendix II shall require the prior grant and presentation of a re-export certificate. A re-export certificate shall only be granted when the following conditions have been met:

   (a) a Management Authority of the State of re-export is satisfied that the specimen was imported into that State in accordance with the provisions of the present Convention; and

   (b) a Management Authority of the State of re-export is satisfied that any living specimen will be so prepared and shipped as to minimize the risk of injury, damage to health or cruel treatment.

6. The introduction from the sea of any specimen of a species included in Appendix II shall require the prior grant of a certificate from a Management Authority of the State of introduction. A certificate shall only be granted when the following conditions have been met:

   (a) a Scientific Authority of the State of introduction advises that the introduction will not be detrimental to the survival of the species involved; and

   (b) a Management Authority of the State of introduction is satisfied that any living specimen will be so handled as to minimize the risk of injury, damage to health or cruel treatment.

7. Certificates referred to in paragraph 6 of this Article may be granted on the advice of a Scientific Authority, in consultation with other national scientific authorities or, when appropriate, international scientific authorities, in respect of periods not exceeding one year for total numbers of specimens to be introduced in such periods.

Article V

Regulation of Trade in Specimens of Species Included in Appendix III

1. All trade in specimens of species included in Appendix III shall be in accordance with the provisions of this Article.
2. The export of any specimen of a species included in Appendix III from any State which has included that species in Appendix III shall require the prior grant and presentation of an export permit. An export permit shall only be granted when the following conditions have been met:
   (a) a Management Authority of the State of export is satisfied that the specimen was not obtained in contravention of the laws of that State for the protection of fauna and flora; and
   (b) a Management Authority of the State of export is satisfied that any living specimen will be so prepared and shipped as to minimize the risk of injury, damage to health or cruel treatment.
3. The import of any specimen of a species included in Appendix III shall require, except in circumstances to which paragraph 4 of this Article applies, the prior presentation of a certificate of origin and, where the import is from a State which has included that species in Appendix III, an export permit.
4. In the case of re-export, a certificate granted by the Management Authority of the State of re-export that the specimen was processed in that State or is being re-exported shall be accepted by the State of import as evidence that the provisions of the present Convention have been complied with in respect of the specimen concerned.

Article VI

Permits and Certificates

1. Permits and certificates granted under the provisions of Articles III, IV and V shall be in accordance with the provisions of this Article.
2. An export permit shall contain the information specified in the model set forth in Appendix IV and may only be used for export within a period of six months from the date on which it was granted.
3. Each permit or certificate shall contain the title of the present Convention, the name and any identifying stamp of the Management Authority granting it and a control number assigned by the Management Authority.
4. Any copies of a permit or certificate issued by a Management Authority shall be clearly marked as copies only and no such copy may be used in

place of the original, except to the extent endorsed thereon.

5. A separate permit or certificate shall be required for each consignment of specimens.

6. A Management Authority of the State of import of any specimen shall cancel and retain the export permit or re-export certificate and any corresponding import permit presented in respect of the import of that specimen.

7. Where appropriate and feasible a Management Authority may affix a mark upon any specimen to assist in identifying the specimen. For these purposes "mark" means any indelible imprint, lead seal or other suitable means of identifying a specimen designed in such a way as to render its imitation by unauthorized persons as difficult as possible.

Article VII

Exemptions and Other Special Provisions Relating to Trade

1. The provisions of Articles III, IV and V shall not apply to the transit or trans-shipment of specimens through or in the territory of a Party while the specimens remain in Customs control.

2. Where a Management Authority of the State of export or re-export is satisfied that a specimen was acquired before the provisions of the present Convention applied to that specimen, the provisions of Articles III, IV and V shall not apply to that specimen where the Management Authority issues a certificate to that effect.

3. The provisions of Articles III, IV and V shall not apply to specimens that are personal or household effects. This exemption shall not apply where:

   (a) in the case of specimens of a species included in Appendix I, they were acquired by the owner outside his State of usual residence and are being imported into that State; or

   (b) in the case of specimens of species included in Appendix II:

   (i) they were acquired by the owner outside his State of usual residence and in a State where removal from the wild occurred;

   (ii) they are being imported into the owner's State of usual residence; and

   (iii) the State where removal from the wild occurred requires the prior grant of export permits before any export of such specimens unless a Management Authority is satisfied that the specimens were acquired before the provisions of the present Convention applied to such specimens.

4. Specimens of an animal species included in Appendix I bred in captivity

for commercial purpose, or of a plant species included in Appendix I artificially propagated for commercial purposes, shall be deemed to be specimens of species included in Appendix II.

5. Where a Management Authority of the State of export is satisfied that any specimen of an animal species was bred in captivity or any specimen of a plant species was artificially propagated, or is a part of such an animal or plant or was derived therefrom, a certificate by that Management Authority to that effect shall be accepted in lieu of any of the permits or certificates required under the provisions of Articles III, IV or V.

6. The provisions of Articles III, IV and V shall not apply to the non-commercial loan, donation or exchange between scientists or scientific institutions registered by a Management Authority of their State, of herbarium specimens, other preserved, dried or embedded museum specimens, and live plant material which carry a label issued or approved by a Management Authority.

7. Articles III, IV and V allow the movement without permits or certificates of specimens which form part of a traveling zoo, circus, menagerie, plant exhibition or other traveling exhibition provided that:
    (a) the exporter or importer registers full details of such specimens with that Management Authority;
    (b) the specimens are in either of the categories specified in paragraph 2 or 5 of this Article; and
    (c) the Management Authority is satisfied that any living specimen will be so transported and cared for as to minimize the risk of injury, damage to health or cruel treatment.

Article VIII

Measures to Be Taken by the Parties

1. The Parties shall take appropriate measures to enforce the provisions of the present Convention and to prohibit trade in specimens in violation thereof. These shall include measures:
    (a) to penalize trade in, or possession of, such specimens, or both; and
    (b) to provide for the confiscation or return to the State of export of such specimens.

2. In addition to the measures taken under paragraph 1 of this Article, a Party may, when it deems it necessary, provide for any method of internal reimbursement for expenses incurred as a result of the confiscation of a specimen traded in violation of the measures taken in the application of the provisions of the present Convention.

3. As far as possible, the Parties shall ensure that specimens shall pass through any formalities required for trade with a minimum of delay. To facilitate such passage, a Party may designate ports of exit and ports of entry at which specimens must be presented for clearance. The Parties shall ensure further that all living specimens, during any period of transit, holding or shipment, are properly cared for so as to minimize the risk of injury, damage to health or cruel treatment.

4. Where a living specimen is confiscated as a result of measures referred to in paragraph 1 of this Article:

    (a) the specimen shall be entrusted to a Management Authority of the State of confiscation;

    (b) the Management Authority shall, after consultation with the State of export, return the specimen to that State at the expense of that State, or to a rescue centre or such other place as the Management Authority deems appropriate and consistent with the purposes of the present Convention; and

    (c) the Management Authority may obtain the advice of a Scientific Authority, or may, whenever it considers it desirable, consult the Secretariat in order to facilitate the decision under sub-paragraph (b) of this paragraph, including the choice of a rescue centre or other place.

5. A rescue centre as referred to in paragraph 4 of this Article means an institution designated by a Management Authority to look after the welfare of living specimens, particularly those that have been confiscated.

6. Each Party shall maintain records of trade in specimens of species included in Appendices I, II and III which shall cover:

    (a) the names and addresses of exporters and importers; and

    (b) the number and type of permits and certificates granted; the States with which such trade occurred; the numbers or quantities and types of specimens; names of species as included in Appendices I, II and III; and, where applicable, the size and sex of the specimens in question.

7. Each Party shall prepare periodic reports on its implementation of the present Convention and shall transmit to the Secretariat:

    (a) an annual report containing a summary of the information specified in sub-paragraph (b) of paragraph 6 of this Article; and

    (b) a biennial report on legislative, regulatory and administrative measures taken to enforce the provisions of the present Convention.

8. The information referred to in paragraph 7 of this Article shall be available to the public where this is not inconsistent with the law of the Party concerned.

Article IX

Management and Scientific Authorities
1. Each Party shall designate for the purpose of the present Convention:
   (a) one or more Management Authorities competent to grant permits or certificates on behalf of that Party; and
   (b) one or more Scientific Authorities.
2. A State depositing an instrument of ratification, acceptance, approval or accession shall at that time inform the Depositary Government of the name and address of the Management Authority authorized to communicate with other Parties and with the Secretariat.
3. Any changes in the designations or authorizations under the provisions of this Article shall be communicated by the Party concerned to the Secretariat for transmission to all other Parties.
4. Any Management Authority referred to in paragraph 2 of this Article shall, if so requested by the Secretariat or the Management Authority of another Party, communicate to it impressions of stamps, seals or other devices used to authenticate permits or certificates.

Article X

Trade with States Not Party to the Convention
Where export or re-export is to, or import is from, a State not a Party to the present Convention, comparable documentation issued by the competent authorities in that State which substantially conforms with the requirements of the present Convention for permits and certificates may be accepted in lieu thereof by any Party.

Article XI

Conference of the Parties
1. The Secretariat shall call a meeting of the Conference of the Parties not later than two years after the entry into force of the present Convention.
2. Thereafter the Secretariat shall convene regular meetings at least once every two years, unless the Conference decides otherwise, and extraordinary meetings at any time on the written request of at least one-third of the Parties.
3. At meetings, whether regular or extraordinary, the Parties shall review the implementation of the present Convention and may:
   (a) make such provision as may be necessary to enable the Secretariat to

carry out its duties;

(b) consider and adopt amendments to Appendices I and II in accordance with Article XV;

(c) review the progress made towards the restoration and conservation of the species included in Appendices I, II and III;

(d) receive and consider any reports presented by the Secretariat or by any Party; and

(e) where appropriate, make recommendations for improving the effectiveness of the present Convention.

4. At each regular meeting, the Parties may determine the time and venue of the next regular meeting to be held in accordance with the provisions of paragraph 2 of this Article.

5. At any meeting, the Parties may determine and adopt rules of procedure for the meeting.

6. The United Nations, its Specialized Agencies and the International Atomic Energy Agency, as well as any State not a Party to the present Convention, may be represented at meetings of the Conference by observers, who shall have the right to participate but not to vote.

7. Any body or agency technically qualified in protection, conservation or management of wild fauna and flora, in the following categories, which has informed the Secretariat of its desire to be represented at meetings of the Conference by observers, shall be admitted unless at least one-third of the Parties present object:

(a) international agencies or bodies, either governmental or non-governmental, and national governmental agencies and bodies; and

(b) national non-governmental agencies or bodies which have been approved for this purpose by the State in which they are located.

Once admitted, these observers shall have the right to participate but not to vote.

Article XII

The Secretariat

1. Upon entry into force of the present Convention, a Secretariat shall be provided by the Executive Director of the United Nations Environment Programme. To the extent and in the manner he considers appropriate, he may be assisted by suitable inter-governmental or non-governmental, international or national agencies and bodies technically qualified in protection, conservation and management of wild fauna and flora.

2. The functions of the Secretariat shall be:
   (a) to arrange for and service meetings of the Parties;
   (b) to perform the functions entrusted to it under the provisions of Articles XV and XVI of the present Convention;
   (c) to undertake scientific and technical studies in accordance with programmes authorized by the Conference of the Parties as will contribute to the implementation of the present Convention, including studies concerning standards for appropriate preparation and shipment of living specimens and the means of identifying specimens;
   (d) to study the reports of Parties and to request from Parties such further information with respect thereto as it deems necessary to ensure implementation of the present Convention;
   (e) to invite the attention of the Parties to any matter pertaining to the aims of the present Convention;
   (f) to publish periodically and distribute to the Parties current editions of Appendices I, II and III together with any information which will facilitate identification of specimens of species included in those Appendices;
   (g) to prepare annual reports to the Parties on its work and on the implementation of the present Convention and such other reports as meetings of the Parties may request;
   (h) to make recommendations for the implementation of the aims and provisions of the present Convention, including the exchange of information of a scientific or technical nature; and
   (i) to perform any other function as may be entrusted to it by the Parties.

Article XIII

International Measures
1. When the Secretariat in the light of information received is satisfied that any species included in Appendices I or II is being affected adversely by trade in specimens of that species or that the provisions of the present Convention are not being effectively implemented, it shall communicate such information to the authorized Management Authority of the Party or Parties concerned.
2. When any Party receives a communication as indicated in paragraph 1 of this Article, it shall, as soon as possible, inform the Secretariat of any relevant facts insofar as its laws permit and, where appropriate, propose remedial action. Where the Party considers that an inquiry is desirable, such inquiry may be carried out by one or more persons expressly authorized by the Party.

3. The information provided by the Party or resulting from any inquiry as specified in paragraph 2 of this Article shall be reviewed by the next Conference of the Parties which may make whatever recommendations it deems appropriate.

Article XIV

Effect on Domestic Legislation and International Conventions

1. The provisions of the present Convention shall in no way affect the right of Parties to adopt:
   (a) stricter domestic measures regarding the conditions for trade, taking, possession or transport of specimens of species included in Appendices I, II and III, or the complete prohibition thereof; or
   (b) domestic measures restricting or prohibiting trade, taking, possession or transport of species not included in Appendices I, II or III.
2. The provisions of the present Convention shall in no way affect the provisions of any domestic measures or the obligations of Parties deriving from any treaty, convention, or international agreement relating to other aspects of trade, taking, possession or transport of specimens which is in force or subsequently may enter into force for any Party including any measure pertaining to the Customs, public health, veterinary or plant quarantine fields.
3. The provisions of the present Convention shall in no way affect the provisions of, or the obligations deriving from, any treaty, convention or international agreement concluded or which may be concluded between States creating a union or regional trade agreement establishing or maintaining a common external Customs control and removing Customs control between the Parties thereto insofar as they relate to trade among the States members of that union agreement.
4. A State Party to the present Convention, which is also a Party to any other treaty, convention or international agreement which is in force at the time of the coming into force of the present Convention and under the provisions of which protection is afforded to marine species included in Appendix II, shall be relieved of the obligation imposed on it under the provisions of the present Convention with respect to trade in specimens of species included in Appendix II that are taken by ships registered in that State and in accordance with the provisions of such other treaty, convention or international agreement.
5. Notwithstanding the provisions of Articles III, IV and V, any export of a specimen taken in accordance with paragraph 4 of this Article shall only

require a certificate from a Management Authority of the State of introduction to the effect that the specimen was taken in accordance with the provisions of the other treaty, convention or international agreement in question.

6. Nothing in the present Convention shall prejudice the codification and development of the law of the sea by the United Nations Conference on the Law of the Sea convened pursuant to Resolution 2750 C(XXV) of the General Assembly of the United Nations nor the present or future claims and legal views of any State concerning the law of the sea and the nature and extent of coastal and flag State jurisdiction.

Article XV

Amendments to Appendices I and II

1. The following provisions shall apply in relation to amendments to Appendices I and II at meetings of the Conference of the Parties:

    (a) Any Party may propose an amendment to Appendix I or II for consideration at the next meeting. The text of the proposed amendment shall be communicated to the Secretariat at least 150 days before the meeting. The Secretariat shall consult the other Parties and interested bodies on the amendment in accordance with the provisions of sub-paragraphs (b) and (c) of paragraph 2 of this Article and shall communicate the response to all Parties not later than 30 days before the meeting.

    (b) Amendments shall be adopted by a two-thirds majority of Parties present and voting. For these purposes, "Parties present and voting" means Parties present and casting an affirmative or negative vote. Parties abstaining from voting shall not be counted among the two-thirds required for adopting an amendment.

    (c) Amendments adopted at a meeting shall enter into force 90 days after that meeting for all Parties except those which make a reservation in accordance with paragraph 3 of this Article.

2. The following provisions shall apply in relation to amendments to Appendices I and II between meetings of the Conference of the Parties:

    (a) Any Party may propose an amendment to Appendix I or II for consideration between meetings by the postal procedures set forth in this paragraph.

    (b) For marine species, the Secretariat shall, upon receiving the text of the proposed amendment, immediately communicate it to the Parties. It shall also consult inter-governmental bodies having a function in relation to those species especially with a view to obtaining scientific data these bodies may be able to provide and to ensuring coordination with any conservation measures enforced by such bodies. The Secretariat shall communicate the views expressed and data provided by these bodies and its own findings and recommendations to the Parties as soon as possible.

(c) For species other than marine species, the Secretariat shall, upon receiving the text of the proposed amendment, immediately communicate it to the Parties, and, as soon as possible thereafter, its own recommendations.

(d) Any Party may, within 60 days of the date on which the Secretariat communicated its recommendations to the Parties under sub-paragraph (b) or (c) of this paragraph, transmit to the Secretariat any comments on the proposed amendment together with any relevant scientific data and information.

(e) The Secretariat shall communicate the replies received together with its own recommendations to the Parties as soon as possible.

(f) If no objection to the proposed amendment is received by the Secretariat within 30 days of the date the replies and recommendations were communicated under the provisions of sub-paragraph (e) of this paragraph, the amendment shall enter into force 90 days later for all Parties except those which make a reservation in accordance with paragraph 3 of this Article.

(g) If an objection by any Party is received by the Secretariat, the proposed amendment shall be submitted to a postal vote in accordance with the provisions of sub-paragraphs (h), (i) and (j) of this paragraph.

(h) The Secretariat shall notify the Parties that notification of objection has been received.

(i) Unless the Secretariat receives the votes for, against or in abstention from at least one-half of the Parties within 60 days of the date of notification under sub-paragraph (h) of this paragraph, the proposed amendment shall be referred to the next meeting of the Conference for further consideration.

(j) Provided that votes are received from one-half of the Parties, the amendment shall be adopted by a two-thirds majority of Parties casting an affirmative or negative vote.

(k) The Secretariat shall notify all Parties of the result of the vote.

(l) If the proposed amendment is adopted, it shall enter into force 90 days after the date of the notification by the Secretariat of its acceptance for all Parties except those which make a reservation in accordance with paragraph 3 of this Article.

3. During the period of 90 days provided for by sub-paragraph (c) of para-

graph 1 or sub-paragraph (1) of paragraph 2 of this Article, any Party may by notification in writing to the Depositary Government make a reservation with respect to the amendment. Until such reservation is withdrawn, the Party shall be treated as a State not a Party to the present Convention with respect to trade in the species concerned.

Article XVI

Appendix III and Amendments Thereto

1. Any party may at any time submit to the Secretariat a list of species which it identifies as being subject to regulation within its jurisdiction for the purpose mentioned in paragraph 3 of Article II. Appendix III shall include the names of the Parties submitting the species for inclusion therein, the scientific names of the species so submitted, and any parts or derivatives of the animals or plants concerned that are specified in relation to the species for the purposes of sub-paragraph (b) of Article I.

2. Each list submitted under the provisions of paragraph 1 of this Article shall be communicated to the Parties by the Secretariat as soon as possible after receiving it. The list shall take effect as part of Appendix III 90 days after the date of such communication. At any time after the communication of such list, any Party may by notification in writing to the Depositary Government enter a reservation with respect to any species or any parts or derivatives, and until such reservation is withdrawn, the State shall be treated as a State not a Party to the present Convention with respect to trade in the species or part or derivative concerned.

3. A Party which has submitted a species for inclusion in Appendix III may withdraw it at any time by notification to the Secretariat which shall communicate the withdrawal to all Parties. The withdrawal shall take effect 30 days after the date of such communication.

4. Any Party submitting a list under the provisions of paragraph 1 of this Article shall submit to the Secretariat a copy of all domestic laws and regulations applicable to the protection of such species, together with any interpretations which the Party may deem appropriate or the Secretariat may request. The Party shall, for as long as the species in question is included in Appendix III, submit any amendment of such laws and regulations or any new interpretations as they are adopted.

Article XVII

Amendment of the Convention

1. An extraordinary meeting of the Conference of the Parties shall be convened by the Secretariat on the written request of at least one-third of the Parties to consider and adopt amendments to the present Convention. Such amendments shall be adopted by a two-thirds majority of Parties present and voting. For these purposes, "Parties present and voting" means Parties present and casting an affirmative or negative vote. Parties abstaining from voting shall not be counted among the two-thirds required for adopting an amendment.

2. The text of any proposed amendment shall be communicated by the Secretariat to all Parties at least 90 days before the meeting.

3. An amendment shall enter into force for the Parties which have accepted it 60 days after two-thirds of the Parties have deposited an instrument of acceptance of the amendment with the Depositary Government. Thereafter, the amendment shall enter into force for any other Party 60 days after that Party deposits its instrument of acceptance of the amendment.

Article XVIII

Resolution of Disputes

1. Any dispute which may arise between two or more Parties with respect to the interpretation or application of the provisions of the present Convention shall be subject to negotiation between the Parties involved in the dispute.

2. If the dispute cannot be resolved in accordance with paragraph 1 of this Article, the Parties may, by mutual consent, submit the dispute to arbitration, in particular that of the Permanent Court of Arbitration at The Hague and the Parties submitting the dispute shall be bound by the arbitral decision.

Article XIX

Signature

The present Convention shall be open for signature at Washington until 30th April 1973 and thereafter at Bern until 31st December 1974.

Article XX

Ratification, Acceptance, Approval
The present Convention shall be subject to ratification, acceptance or approval. Instruments of ratification, acceptance or approval shall be deposited with the Government of the Swiss Confederation which shall be the Depositary Government.

Article XXI

Accession
The present Convention shall be open indefinitely for accession. Instruments of accession shall be deposited with the Depositary Government.

Article XXII

Entry into Force
1. The present Convention shall enter into force 90 days after the date of deposit of the tenth instrument of ratification, acceptance, approval or accession with the Depositary Government.
2. For each State which ratifies, accepts or approves the present Convention or accedes thereto after the deposit of the tenth instrument of ratification, acceptance, approval or accession, the present Convention shall enter into force 90 days after the deposit by such State of its instrument of ratification, acceptance, approval or accession.

Article XXIII

Reservations
1. The provisions of the present Convention shall not be subject to general reservations. Specific reservations may be entered in accordance with the provisions of this Article and Articles XV and XVI.
2. Any State may, on depositing its instrument of ratification, acceptance, approval or accession, enter a specific reservation with regard to:
   (a) any species included in Appendix I, II or III; or
   (b) any parts or derivatives specified in relation to a species concluded in Appendix III.
3. Until a Party withdraws its reservation entered under the provisions of this Article, it shall be treated as a State not a Party to the present Convention with respect to trade in the particular species or parts or derivatives specified in such reservation.

Article XXIV

Denunciation
Any Party may denounce the present Convention by written notification to the Depositary Government at any time. The denunciation shall take effect twelve months after the Depositary Government has received the notification.

Article XXV

Depositary
1. The original of the present Convention, in the Chinese, English, French, Russian and Spanish languages, each version being equally authentic, shall be deposited with the Depositary Government, which shall transmit certified copies thereof to all States that have signed it or deposited instruments of accession to it.
2. The Depositary Government shall inform all signatory and acceding States and the Secretariat of signatures, deposit of instruments of ratification, acceptance, approval or accession, entry into force of the present Convention, amendments thereto, entry and withdrawal of reservations and notifications of denunciation.
3. As soon as the present Convention enters into force, a certified copy thereof shall be transmitted by the Depositary Government to the Secretariat of the United Nations for registration and publication in accordance with Article 102 of the Charter of the United Nations.

In witness whereof the undersigned Plenipotentiaries, being duly authorized to that effect, have signed the present Convention.

Done at Washington this third day of March, One Thousand Nine Hundred and Seventy-three.

* * *

Editor's note: Appendices I, II, and III are in Appendix A to this book, pp. 59–118. Appendix IV is not included.

3/Species and Trade

RHINOCEROS TRADE

The five species of rhinoceros are classified in the family Rhinocerotidae under the order Perissodactyla. The black rhino (*Diceros bicornis*) and the white rhino (*Ceratotherium simum*) are found in Africa, while the Indian or greater one-horned rhino (*Rhinoceros unicornis*), the Javan rhino (*Rhinoceros sondaicus*), and the Sumatran rhino (*Dicerorhinus sumatrensis*) are all found in Asia.

Black rhino (*Diceros bicornis*). Photo by Rick Weyerhaueser.

Status

Since 1970, more than 90 percent of the world's rhinos have disappeared. Asian species are in the most precarious situation: Wild population estimates are fewer than 2,000 for the Indian rhino, 400 to 500 for the Sumatran rhino, and fewer than 100 for the Javan rhino. In Africa, black rhino populations have declined to perhaps 2,000—a decrease of 95 percent since 1970. Roughly 5,900 white rhinos, mostly in South Africa, remain in the wild. A growing problem for all rhinos is increased population fragmentation.

Rhinos are killed primarily for their valuable horns, but also for their hides, hooves, and other body parts. In Yemen, rhino horns are carved into ceremonial dagger handles, known as jambiyyas. In many Asian communities, people consume ground rhino horn for fever reduction and other remedies and use rhino hide and urine for other medicinal purposes—practices that have persisted for centuries. (Contrary to popular belief, rhino horn derivatives are seldom used as aphrodisiacs.)

Trade Protection

All rhino products and derivatives are prohibited from commercial international trade under Appendix I of CITES, which prohibits all commercial trade in species on that list. The U.S. Endangered Species Act also prohibits the import of, and interstate commerce in, rhinos and rhino products in the United States, although southern white rhino trophies may be imported with proper permits from South Africa where the rhino population is considered stable to increasing. With the possible exceptions of Cambodia and Laos, rhinos receive legal protection from poaching and illicit trade in countries throughout their range.

Effects of Trade

The vast majority of rhino horn on the market today comes from the black rhino, which recently has been killed mostly in Zimbabwe and traded through surrounding countries. The principal consuming nations are China, South Korea, Taiwan, and Yemen. All of these countries have legal restrictions on the international trade of rhino horn, but the prohibitions are not well enforced. Of the four principal consuming nations, China and Korea are members of CITES.

In Africa, surveys indicate that, since 1980, most of the black rhino population has disappeared from its former range. Black rhinos are nearly gone from Angola, Chad, Ethiopia, Malawi, Mozambique, Rwanda, Somalia, Sudan, and Zambia. Populations in Tanzania and Zimbabwe have also been severely threatened by poaching, which is especially acute in the Zambezi Valley of Zimbabwe along the border with Zambia. In contrast, the southern white rhino of South Africa has experienced a population increase largely as a result of years of effective protection and management. Only the rhino populations of Kenya, Namibia, and South Africa are currently considered relatively safe from poaching. Recent increases in poaching of the Indian rhino in India and Nepal have depleted some populations of the species.

Rhino horn brings remarkable prices on the east Asian market. In the wholesale markets of Taiwan, prices for the more valuable Asian species range from $10,000 to upwards of $30,000 per kilo. African rhino horn sells for about $1,000 to $1,500 per kilo wholesale in that market. Profits from the sale of rhino horn are so great that poachers, smugglers, and shop owners will risk fines, jail sentences, and even death.

Enforcement activities and emergency measures such as rhino translocation have helped to deter illegal hunting in some areas. Nevertheless, poaching still exacts a large toll. Because of the high profits involved in the sale of rhino products and the lack of political will in major consuming nations, trade bans around the world have been difficult to enforce.

During the 1970s, an estimated 17,600 kilos of rhino horn were traded annually worldwide. During the 1980s, the figure dropped to an estimated 6,600 kilos per year. An average black rhino horn weighs about 6 pounds, while an average Javan rhino horn weighs about one-half pound.

Conservation Measures

Stopping the rhino trade problem requires multiple actions on all fronts, increased international funding, and new, creative initiatives. Publicity on the plight of the rhinos should continue to be directed toward consumer nations, and users of traditional oriental medicines should continue to explore possible alternative substitute materials like water buffalo horns, which are available. CITES parties should recruit all nonmembers to join the treaty, encourage better enforcement of existing bans, and urge establishment of new rhino horn trade restrictions and trade control regimes. African and Asian nations also need international assistance to increase their anti-poaching forces, establish well-protected rhino sanctuaries, and strengthen efforts to protect the rhino's habitat.

TIGER TRADE

The largest member of the cat family Felidae, the tiger (*Panthera tigris*) is one of the world's most threatened carnivores. Primarily an Asian species, the tiger ranges from the Indian subcontinent through Southeast Asia to the Russian Far East.

Status

Bengal tiger (*Panthera tigris tigris*).
Photo by Peter Jackson.

Of any predator, tigers require the largest land area to survive and must compete with man for limited habitat and resources. Habitat fragmentation is a severe threat to the tiger's survival. In the last century, three subspecies of tiger became extinct: the Caspian tiger (*P.t. virgata*), the Javan tiger (*P.t. sondaica*), and the Bali tiger (*P.t. balica*). The five subspecies that survive today include the Siberian (also called the Manchurian or Amur) tiger (*P.t. altaica*), which numbers an estimated 200–250 in the wild; the South China or Amoy tiger (*P.t. amoyensis*), with fewer than 50 left; the Indo-Chinese tiger (*P.t. corbetti*), with 800 to 1,200 remaining; the Bengal or Indian tiger (*P.t. tigris*), numbering between 2,900 and 4,500; and the Sumatran tiger (*P.t. sumatrae*), numbering between 250 and 400 in the wild.

Illegal hunting threatens many populations. Tigers are hunted to produce exotic souvenirs (skins, stuffed heads, etc.) for tourists and for use of their body parts in oriental medicinals. Tiger bones are used in oriental medicine to treat such symptoms as joint pain and stiffness, muscular weakness, back pain, paralysis, and muscular spasms. Other tiger parts that are used medicinally include the tail, which is mixed with soap to treat skin diseases; whiskers, which are used as a charm for protection and to lend courage; the penis, which is used as an aphrodisiac; and the brain, which is used as a body rub to cure acne. Many Asian countries have for centuries used animal parts for medicinal purposes, and a belief in their efficacy for treating illnesses is deeply rooted in local cultures.

Trade Protection

The tiger is listed on Appendix I of CITES, which prohibits all commercial trade in species on that list. In addition, the U.S. Endangered Species Act prohibits the import of, and interstate commerce in, tiger products in the United States. Virtually all countries where tigers live have protection laws in place, although enforcement varies significantly from country to country. Commerce in tigers for circuses and zoos is mostly legal and usually involves captive-bred animals.

Effects of Trade

Much like rhinos, bears, and other endangered species in Asia, tigers are killed because their body parts command high prices from smugglers and medicinal traders. In Russia, a single poached tiger is so valuable that it could reportedly be exchanged for two or three pickup trucks in 1992. A tiger pelt may bring up to $8,000 in a tourist shop in some Asian countries, while tiger bone sells for between $800 and $1,200 per kilogram in the Taiwanese retail market. Depending on its size, an individual adult tiger yields between 6 and 11 kilograms of dried bone.

Most of the illegal trade in tiger parts occurs in the tiger's historic range in Asia. The People's Republic of China, South Korea, Taiwan, India, Nepal, Thailand, Vietnam, Cambodia, Laos, and Burma all have serious poaching and illegal trade problems. The principal tiger consuming countries are China, South Korea, and Taiwan, the latter two of which do not have native tiger populations. Tiger products are also consumed throughout Asia and other parts of the world, including the United States, where there are growing east Asian communities.

Tiger poaching has increased dramatically in the last five years with demand for tiger products in the major consuming countries apparently increasing as a result of growing human populations and increasing personal wealth. India, home to at least two-thirds of the world's tigers, has been particularly hard hit with an average 350 tigers lost to poachers each year from 1989 to 1993. The dwindling

Siberian or Amur tiger population has also suffered severe losses—a problem that has been aggravated by the breakup of the former Soviet Union.

Conservation Measures

Although habitat loss and fragmentation are the greatest long-term threats to the tiger, the most immediate concerns are rampant poaching and illegal trade. Stopping the illegal tiger trade requires actions on several fronts. CITES parties must urge members to enforce the treaty in their countries and must urge non-member states to join CITES. Assistance to expand anti-poaching operations and habitat protection programs in tiger-range nations must also be provided, and countries where tiger parts are sold illegally must clamp down on this commerce. A major problem has been the lack of political will in consumer countries to stop the illegal trade.

Publicity about tiger poaching must continue to be directed to those countries that currently use large quantities of tiger bone and other parts. Those countries and their medical communities must also be encouraged to use as medicines alternatives and synthetic products that are equally effective at treating the illnesses for which tiger parts are used. Tourists should be discouraged from buying tiger trinkets made from teeth and claws, tiger pelts, and stuffed heads and, where possible, report such sales to local and international authorities. Increased international funding to help build and strengthen protected areas and national parks where tigers live is also essential to the tiger's survival.

ELEPHANT IVORY TRADE

The two species of elephant are classified in the order Proboscidea. Elephants are the largest living land animals with adults reaching 4 meters in height and weighing up to 7,500 kg. Both the Asian and African species inhabit forests, savannahs, and river valleys and live in herds made up of complex family units. Elephants require extensive land areas and vegetation to survive. Adults consume 150 to 170 kilos of grasses, trees, and shrubs daily. Both species of elephant have been valued and hunted for centuries for their ivory tusks. Male and female African elephants carry ivory, while only male Asian elephants have tusks.

African elephants (*Loxodonta africana*).
Photo by Jorgen Thomsen/WWF.

Status

The estimated 29,000 to 44,000 Asian elephants that remain in the wild are found only in isolated areas of India, continental Southeast Asia, the Malay Peninsula, Sri Lanka, Sumatra, Borneo, and the Andaman Islands in the Bay of Bengal off the coast of India. The African elephant currently exists in much of sub-Saharan Africa with a range—although increasingly fragmented—extending through more than 30 countries. Although the African elephant is more numerous than the Asian elephant, the species underwent a dramatic decline in the 1970s and 1980s as a result of poaching for the ivory trade. There were about 1.2 million African elephants in the late 1970s, but only an estimated 600,000 remain today. Of those, roughly 45 percent can be found in the rain forests of central Africa, 30 percent in southern Africa, 20 percent in eastern Africa, and fewer than 5 percent in western Africa.

Elephant losses to poaching in the 1980s were especially acute in the Central African Republic, Kenya, Mozambique, Somalia, Sudan, Tanzania, and Zaire. Poaching increased in the late 1970s and 1980s as a result of many factors, including the widespread availability of automatic weapons in parts of Africa, which increased poaching efficiency; unstable economies and the need for new sources of foreign exchange that ivory provided; and political corruption in some areas. A 1990 international ban on the ivory trade adopted by CITES, coupled with increasing support for anti-poaching efforts, has helped to reduce poaching in many areas of Africa.

Trade Protection

Both the Asian and African elephants are listed on Appendix I of CITES, which prohibits all commercial trade in species on that list. In addition, the Asian elephant is listed as "endangered" and the African elephant as "threatened" under the U.S. Endangered Species Act. The Endangered Species Act prohibits the import of, and interstate commerce in, products of all species listed as endangered. The African Elephant Conservation Act, passed in 1988, allows the U.S. government to take strict action against illegal ivory imports and authorizes U.S. government funding for elephant field conservation projects. Under this law, the United States banned imports of African elephant ivory in 1989. Within the United States, however, it is legal to buy, sell, and transport African elephant ivory. Both CITES and U.S. law allow for limited trade of noncommercial sport-hunted elephant trophies from approved countries. Under the African Elephant Conservation Act, the United States currently provides more than $1 million to elephant conservation projects in Africa.

Effects of Trade

During the few years before the January 1990 listing of the African elephant on Appendix I of CITES, continued legal and illegal annual ivory exports from Africa averaged between 700 and 800 metric tons—the equivalent of about 75,000 dead elephants and a level far greater than the elephant population could sustain. The largest importers of ivory from Africa were Hong Kong and Japan, which together accounted for about 75 percent of total imports. The United States imported far more worked ivory products than raw ivory in the 1980s. In 1988, more than $20 million worth of commercial ivory products, mostly jewelry, entered the United States, primarily from Hong Kong.

Effects of the Ivory Ban

The international ban on ivory trade has had a dramatic effect on world commerce in ivory. The U.S. market has been virtually shut down, and prices have fallen on other world markets and in Africa. Poaching has also declined overall, although recent reports indicate increased poaching activity in some parts of Africa, particularly in areas of civil unrest and along unstable political boundries. International conservation efforts now focus on ivory trade control, protected area development, anti-poaching activities, and careful management of elephants to avoid increased conflict with human populations.

Some African nations, particularly South Africa, Zimbabwe, and Botswana, have management programs that have been relatively effective at controlling poaching and fostering healthy elephant populations. In some parts of these countries, the governments have determined that elephant numbers exceed the carrying capacity of the land and require control through limited culling, or selective thinning, of the herds.

Other Threats

In the 1970s and 1980s, the demand for ivory was the most serious threat to the survival of the African elephant. However, as human populations increase throughout Africa, elephants—which require enormous food resources and large land areas in which to live—are forced into greater competition for food, water, and habitat. The African elephant is losing ground, and the problem is exacerbated by a paucity of wildlife management programs in many African nations.

Conservation Measures

Although the global movement that eventually shut down the international trade in ivory in the late 1980s has helped save many elephants, its benefits will be short-lived unless conservationists succeed in turning widespread public passion and commitment to elephants into constructive efforts within Africa itself. Conservationists must continue to help African nations develop and implement programs that meet Africa's needs. Consumers in the developed world must stay informed about the status of the African elephant and refrain from buying ivory products.

BEAR TRADE

Bears are classified in the family Ursidae under the order Carnivora. Scientists recognize eight species of bear: the sun bear *(Helarctos malayanus)*, the sloth bear *(Melursus ursinus)*, and Asiatic black bear *(Ursus thibetanus)* of Asia; the brown bear *(U. arctos)* of Eurasia and North America; the American black bear *(U. americanus)* of North America; the polar bear *(U. maritimus)* of polar regions; the giant panda *(Ailuropoda melanoleuca)* of China; and the spectacled bear *(Tremarctos ornatus)* of the Andean region of South America. Bears inhabit every continent except Australia and Antarctica.

American Black Bear *(Ursus americanus)*.
Photo by George W. Frame/WWF.

Status

All bear species, except for the polar bear, the American black bear, and the Alaskan and Canadian populations of the brown bear, have experienced dramatic population declines in recent decades. The sun bear, Asiatic black bear, most populations of the brown bear, and sloth bear have probably suffered the most significant declines in recent decades. Scientists estimate that close to 600,000 American black bears still inhabit their range throughout North America. Sloth bears, however, number fewer than 10,000, while probably no more than 1,000 giant pandas survive in the wild in China.

As with most large carnivores, bear populations have declined primarily due to habitat loss and human persecution. Because bear gallbladders bring high prices on the international market, bears are also killed for their body parts. Indeed, many bear species are increasingly being killed solely for their gallbladders.

In much of Asia, many bear populations have been pushed to the brink of extinction. Although most black and brown bear populations in North America are not considered endangered, poaching has increased in some areas because of the growing demand for bear parts. In parts of Asia, eastern Europe, the former Soviet Union, and South America, habitat destruction and illegal hunting and trade have led to serious population declines of native bears. In recent years, in particular, the breakdown of wildlife law enforcement in the former Soviet Union has led to increased poaching of brown bears. China, South Korea, and Taiwan are the principal import markets for bear parts, particularly gallbladders.

Trade Protection

The Asiatic black bear, sun bear, sloth bear, giant panda, spectacled bear, and certain populations of brown bear are listed on Appendix I of CITES, which prohibits all commercial trade in species on that list. All other species are listed on Appendix II of CITES, which regulates commercial trade through a permit system. In addition, the U.S. Endangered Species Act restricts commerce in grizzly bears (*U. arctos horribilis*) from the lower 48 states. The Endangered Species Act also prohibits U.S. trade in some listed nonnative brown bear subspecies from Eurasia and Mexico. The U.S. Marine Mammal Protection Act prohibits trade in the polar bear, except for certain subsistence uses by American Indians and some noncommercial sport-hunted trophies.

Many foreign laws also regulate or prohibit hunting and trade of native bears. In countries where the sale of bear parts is illegal or restricted, the profits to be gained are so great that poachers, dealers, and traditional medicine shop owners will risk jail sentences and fines to buy or sell bear parts. In many Asian countries, the use of bear gallbladders is deeply rooted in traditional medicinal practices. Thus, although commerce in protected species' gallbladders may be restricted or prohibited, many existing laws often are not enforced.

Effects of Trade

In Taiwan a bear gallbladder of average weight is worth $800 to $3,000. The bile salts of bear gallbladders are used in various remedies for the traditional oriental medicinal market. According to Asian medical practitioners, bile salts can cure various intestinal, liver, fever, and cardiac-related illnesses. Research has shown that gallbladder derivatives have efficacy as an antispasmodic, poison antidote, antihypertensive, or anti-coughing agent. Despite popular western belief, bear gallbladders are not used as aphrodisiacs. Bear paws, claws, teeth, and fur are also traded in Asian, North American, and European markets. A bowl of bear paw soup fetches up to $1,500 in some upscale Taiwanese restaurants that cater to wealthy clients seeking to dine on unusual or endangered animals.

At least 18 Asian countries are known to trade commercially in bear parts. Because native bears in many of those countries have been hunted to dangerously low levels, bear parts are increasingly being imported from around the world, particularly North America. Of the world's eight bear species, the giant panda of the People's Republic of China remains the only species not hunted specifically for its gallbladder. However, the panda is severely threatened by habitat loss, human encroachment in panda reserves, capture of live animals for zoos, and hunting for a select Asian curio market.

Conservation Measures

If the trade in bear parts, particularly in gallbladders, is to be controlled, action must occur on several fronts. At present, there are still legal markets for bear parts in some states in the United States and in some Canadian territories or provinces. Both the United States and Canada must ensure that there are strong safeguards to prevent "laundering" of bear parts taken in states or provinces that prohibit such trade.

Asian countries trading bear gallbladders must greatly strengthen their enforcement efforts to ensure that imports are only from legally hunted and traded bears. Chemical substitutes for bear bile salts that are available to Asian consumers should be promoted and encouraged by the governments and medical communities of the major consumer nations. To help reduce the demand for bear gallbladders, Asian countries that import gallbladders and bile salts should make a greater effort to educate consumers about the efficacy of chemical substitutes.

PRIMATE TRADE

Scientists recognize about 200 different species of nonhuman primates, classified in the order Primates. Most of these are distributed throughout the tropical rain forests of Africa, Asia, and Latin America. The close biological relationship of nonhuman primates to human beings makes nonhuman primates desirable as models for biomedical research. Primates are also sought by zoological parks, and many are popular, although often illegal, pets in some parts of the world. Primates are also an important source of protein for people in certain countries, particularly in parts of Africa and the Amazon region of South America.

Rhesus macaque (*Macaca mulatta*).
Photo by by Russell Mittermeier.

The majority of primates in trade today are Old World species. The species most heavily used by biomedical researchers are the crab-eating (long-tail) macaque (*Macaca fascicularis*), the pigtail macaque (*M. nemestrina*), and the rhesus macaque (*M. mulatta*) from Asia. Researchers also use anubis baboons (*Papio anubis*) and savannah (green) monkeys (*Cercopithicus aethiops*) from Africa and owl or night monkeys (*Aotus spp.*), capuchins (*Cebus spp.*), and squirrel monkeys (*Saimiri spp.*) from the New World tropics.

Status

Many primates are in danger of extinction. The chimpanzee (*Pan troglodytes*) of west and central Africa, the mountain gorilla (*Gorilla gorilla beringei*) of central Africa, the golden lion tamarin (*Leontophitecus rosalia*) of Brazil, the yellow-tailed woolly monkey (*Lagothrix flavicauda*) of Peru, the cotton-topped tamarin (*Saguinus bicolor*) of Colombia, and the indri (*Indri indri*) and aye aye (*Daubentonia madagascariensis*) of Madagascar are just a few of the species that face extinction. Many populations of other species and subspecies of wild primates are declining in the face of widespread destruction of tropical rain forests, which are home to 90 percent of all primates.

The greatest factors in population declines among wild primates are destruction of tropical forests for agriculture, grazing, and other human development interests, coupled with poor management and protection of existing parks and reserves. Local hunting for food and international trade also threatens certain species. Western nations are importing fewer primates for pets than they once did, but local pet trade continues in developing countries. The steady global demand for chimpanzees in medical research recently prompted the United States to uplist this species from "threatened" to "endangered" under the U.S. Endangered Species Act.

Trade Protection

Sixty-one primate species and 6 subspecies are listed on Appendix I of CITES, which prohibits all commercial trade in species on that list. All other primate species are listed on Appendix II of CITES, which regulates commercial trade through a permit system. In addition, the United States prohibits importation of primates as pets under a U.S. Public Health Service regulation adopted in 1975. Under the U.S. Endangered Species Act, 58 primate species and 5 subspecies are listed as "endangered," and 13 species are listed as "threatened."

Effects of Trade

Because statistics are often unreliable, the total volume of world trade is difficult to determine. Reported world imports were about 25,000 to 30,000 live primates annually in the late 1980s. Over the last two decades global trade appears to have declined. Recent instances of illegal trade in endangered primates such as the chimpanzee (Pan troglodytes), orangutan (Pongo pygmaeus), golden lion tamarin (Leontophitecus rosalia), and drill (Papio leucophaeus) have alarmed conservationists worldwide. These instances indicate that, although illicit trade channels may be gradually closing down, demand continues for certain species, especially those with high value on the live animal market.

The Philippines, Indonesia, Mauritius, and China export large numbers of macaques. Kenya, Tanzania, Ethiopia, St. Kitts, and Barbados are principal suppliers of savannah (green) monkeys and baboons to the world market. (The latter two countries have introduced populations of non-native green monkeys.) Guyana, Peru, and Brazil are currently the primary sources of New World species—notably squirrel, night, and capuchin monkeys—that enter trade. The principal importing countries are Canada, France, Japan, the Netherlands, Taiwan, the United Kingdom, and the United States.

The world's largest importer of primates, the United States imported 10,000 to 15,000 live animals per year over the last decade, primarily for research purposes. Since the mid-1960s, imports have declined overall with a sharp decline in 1990 attributable to stricter quarantine requirements. Since then, however, imports have gone up as a result of expanding biomedical research demands, including AIDS research. Due partly to increased availability of captive-bred primates, such as rhesus macaques, squirrel monkeys, baboons, crab-eating macaques, and owl monkeys, perhaps 55,000 primates per year are in circulation within the United States. The United States also exports primates. For the period 1984–89, exports averaged about 800 annually.

Conservation Measures

Because many species that inhabit tropical forest regions are extremely sensitive to habitat disturbance, habitat preservation is the most important measure for long-term conservation of primates in the world. In addition, better enforcement of existing trade and hunting laws will help to ensure the existence of primates in areas where tropical forests remain intact.

PARROT TRADE

Parrots, or psittacines, are classified in the order Psittaciformes. Commonly called parakeets, macaws, cockatoos, rosellas, amazons, conures, or lorikeets, all parrots are easily identified by a characteristic downward-curving beak and often brightly colored plumage. Because of their beauty, intelligence, and longevity, parrots are in great demand as pets.

Status

There are approximately 330 parrot species worldwide, of which at least 40 are

considered to be in danger of extinction, largely because of habitat loss and excessive trade in certain countries. Endangered species include the Puerto Rican parrot (*Amazona vittata*), the imperial parrot (*Amazona imperialis*) from the Caribbean island of Dominica, the hyacinth macaw (*Anodorhynchus hyacinthinus*) and the Buffon's macaw (*Ara ambigua*) from Latin America, and the palm cockatoo (*Prosciger aterrimus*) from New Guinea and Australia.

Australian King Parrot (*Alisterus scapularis*).
Photo by Mauri Rautkari/WWF.

Trade Protection

All but two parrot species are protected under CITES. About 40 species considered to be endangered are listed on CITES Appendix I, which prohibits all commercial trade in species on that list. Virtually all other parrots are listed on Appendix II of CITES, which regulates commercial trade through a permit system. CITES does not regulate trade in the budgerigar (*Melopsittacus undulatus*) and the cockatiel (*Nymphicus hollandicus*), which are commonly bred in captivity. Most Appendix I parrot species are also listed as "endangered" under the U.S. Endangered Species Act and are prohibited from both interstate and international trade. In addition, the U.S. Lacey Act declares it illegal to import species that are protected from trade in their country of origin. U.S. import regulations also require a 30-day quarantine of all psittacines at government-approved stations to screen for health problems and to protect native birds and poultry from two very contagious diseases: psittacosis and exotic Newcastle disease (VVND). In 1992, the U.S. government adopted the Wild Bird Conservation Act, which prohibits the commercial import of almost all wild parrots for the pet trade, except from countries with approved management and conservation programs and from approved captive breeding facilities.

Effects of Trade

In 1990, at least 150,000 of the 450,000 live birds imported into the United States were parrots. Japan and several European countries—notably Belgium, the Netherlands, Germany, and the United Kingdom—are also major importers. Despite the difficulty and expense sometimes involved in keeping large parrots in captivity, macaws and cockatoos have become particularly popular with U.S. bird lovers. With strict laws now in place in the United States, parrot imports have declined considerably, and captive breeding is on the increase.

Since passage of the Wild Bird Conservation Act, U.S. imports of parrots have slowed to a trickle. Non-CITES bird species, such as finches, now dominate the import trade. In the past, the vast majority of parrots imported into the United States came from wild populations. Depending on the species, mortality suffered during capture, transit, and quarantine can range from 5 to 80 percent. Because large parrots, such as macaws and cockatoos, do not produce large numbers of offspring and cannot rebuild their wild populations quickly, excessive trade for some species has been devastating. In addition, many of the the most sought after species are also the most threatened. Many parrot species are naturally rare in the wild and are especially vulnerable to excessive capture for trade.

The illicit trade in parrots involves both smuggling and laundering or falsification of shipping documents. Sometimes smuggled out of countries like Australia, Brazil, or Ghana that restrict their export, parrots are brought into nearby trade centers, such as Singapore, Argentina, or the Ivory Coast, where export is allowed or where falsified permits can sometimes be obtained. Parrots are also occasionally smuggled into countries with strict import and quarantine laws. In the late 1980s, at least 50,000 birds, mostly parrots, were believed to be smuggled into the United States each year. Most of them came across the vast U.S.-Mexico border. It appears that smuggling across the U.S.-Mexico border may be increasing.

Since the late 1980s, major suppliers of Latin American parrot species have been Argentina, Guyana, Honduras, Nicaragua, and Peru. Asian species have come to the United States mainly from Indonesia. African species are imported from Senegal, Tanzania, Cameroon, and Mali. Because of the difficulties in controlling illegal trade, export rules in countries of origin change frequently; and patterns of trade differ from year to year. Most of the captive-bred species imported by the United States are Australian, Asian, or African species that are bred primarily in Belgium and the Netherlands.

Parrots, particularly the large, rare species, can fetch steep prices on the international market. A hyacinth macaw can sell for up to $8,000, while a breeding pair of palm cockatoos can sell for more than $30,000. Some of the most popular "talking" parrots, such as the yellow-naped Amazon and the African grey parrot, sell for $300 to $1,000 on the U.S. market. Both of these species have been subject to extensive illegal trade in the recent past, but both species are also increasingly bred in captivity.

Conservation Measures

As human populations increase worldwide, parrots and other species are forced into greater competition for space and resources. Trade generally adds to these stresses. In addition, many laws protecting psittacines are poorly enforced. Better management of the natural areas in which parrots live and better application of conservation laws and trade controls will help to ensure their continued survival.

A number of exporting countries, such as Guyana and Indonesia, have established export quotas under CITES in an attempt to limit trade while scientific studies are carried out to determine the status of species in the wild. Much has yet to be learned about the natural history of many parrot species and the impact of trade on populations. In addition, as a result of public concern over the mortality suffered in shipping, many airlines no longer transport commercial shipments of live birds.

For consumers who wish to own a parrot, captive-bred species are often the best choice because they generally enter trade legally and are usually healthier and tamer than their wild counterparts. The only two non-CITES-regulated parrots available in pet stores, the cockatiel and budgerigar or budgie, are widely bred in captivity.

As U.S. imports of wild-caught parrot species decline, increasing numbers of captive-bred parrots are becoming available to consumers. Some captive-bred species include the peach-faced lovebird (*Agapornis roseicollis*), ring-necked parakeet (*Psittacula krameri*), sun conure (*Aratinga solstitailis*), and blue and gold macaw (*Ara ararauna*).

F
LOWER BULB TRADE

Flower bulbs constitute a large and growing share of the international ornamental plant trade. Since the early 1980s, there has been a surge in demand in the United States: More than 1 billion bulbs were imported in 1990, compared with about 550 million in 1982. This substantial jump in U.S. imports has resulted primarily from an increase in low-cost, mass-produced exports from the Netherlands where propagation and trade in flower bulbs is a well-established industry.

Status

Conservationists have become increasingly concerned over the growing trade of wild-collected bulbs originating from the Mediterranean region—especially Turkey, Portugal, and Spain. In Turkey, where horticultural trade to western Europe has persisted for centuries, commercial collection of some bulb species poses a severe threat to wild populations. Each year, tens of millions of winter aconite (*Eranthis*), *Cyclamen*, *Anemone*, snowdrops (*Galanthus*), and other attractive bulb species leave Turkey for the Netherlands where wholesalers sort and auction them to buyers for propagation and reexport. The bulb trade from Portugal and Spain also involves large quantities of wild-collected species, especially *Narcissus*.

Snowdrops *(Galanthus)*. Photo by Nina Marshall/WWF.

Gardeners often claim planting bulbs at home in their gardens helps to preserve endangered bulbs. Unfortunately, continued commercial exploitation of wild-collected bulbs depletes the gene pool in native habitats and diminishes the likelihood that bulb populations can survive in the wild.

Trade Protection

Several flower-bulb species are protected both by domestic legislation in their countries of origin and by international agreements. Species in the genera *Cyclamen, Galanthus, Sternbergia,* and *Cypripedium* (lady slipper orchids) have been listed on Appendix II of CITES, which regulates commercial trade through a permit system. Recently, the European Union has taken measures to strengthen protection for CITES-listed species through a special regulation that prohibits all trade in three *Cyclamen* species traded within the EU. Austria, France, Germany, Greece, Ireland, Italy, Switzerland, and the United States also protect some bulb species from collection in the wild. However, two of the most important countries involved in the wild bulb trade—Spain and Portugal—do not yet adequately protect their native bulb flora.

Effects of Trade

With 75 to 80 percent of world trade and exports of more than 10 billion bulbs annually, the Netherlands dominates the international flower bulb industry. Other major suppliers to the world market include Belgium, Canada, France, India, Israel, Japan, Portugal, South Africa, Spain, Turkey, and the United Kingdom. The United States also produces millions of flower bulbs each year for the domestic market, but this quantity represents a much smaller volume than U.S. imports.

Bulbs, especially those labeled "wild," "species," or "botanicals," often originate in the wild. (The term bulb includes underground plant storage structures such as corms, tubers, true bulbs, and rhizomes.) Examples of such wild species in trade include snowdrops *(Galanthus spp.)*; winter aconite *(Eranthis hyemalis)*; some *Narcissus* species, particularly angel's tears *(Narcissus triandrus albus)*, *N. asturiensis*, and *N. cyclamineus*; summer snowflake *(Leocojum aestivum)*; the sea daffodil *(Pancratium maritimum)*; *Sternbergia* species; *Cyclamen* species (except *L. persicum*); and some *Crocus* species.

Tens of thousands of hybrid cultivars make up the vast majority of the flower bulbs in trade. Bulbs bearing such names as "February Gold," "Triumph," and *Narcissus* "Cora Ann," for example, represent artificially propagated cultivars that can be bought and sold without harming wild populations.

It is often difficult to tell if bulbs have been uprooted in the wild, although shape, texture, and color help to indicate the source for some species. For example, wild-collected bulbs from such genera as *Arum* and *Cyclamen* are coarse and often misshapen from rough handling or from growing between rocks. Wild *Fritillaria* bulbs become easily bruised and damaged during collection and handling, whereas cultivated stock is generally evenly shaped and unblemished.

Conservation Measures

Although domestic legislation and international treaties need to be strengthened and extended to cover a wider range of species in trade, these measures alone cannot curtail the destructive trade in wild-collected species. In May 1990, the Netherlands bulb industry, working with conservation organizations, agreed to implement a labeling system for bulbs that provides customers with information about the origin of the bulbs they purchase. All wild bulbs, such as snowdrops and winter daffodils, are required to be labeled "bulbs from wild source." All propagated minor bulbs are now required to be labeled "bulbs grown from cultivated stock." The agreement, which will be extended in 1995 to include all bulbs (hybrids, varieties, and cultivars) exported from the Netherlands, is being monitored by conservation organizations. A 1993 survey conducted by TRAFFIC and U.S. retail nursery outlets indicated that a number of minor bulbs of Dutch origin were unlabeled.

In addition to strengthened legislation, nations are turning their efforts to developing and promoting the propagation of bulbs for export. Turkey, for example, has begun to set up indigenous propagation projects to cultivate a variety of native bulb species such as *Galanthus*, *Eranthis*, and *Fritillaria*. Because of the length of time it takes for some species to grow from seed to salable size, these efforts are not expected to provide cultivated bulbs before 1995.

Consumers can play a more active role in slowing the detrimental trade in wild species. If bulb shoppers do not find labels on bulbs from the Netherlands, they should inquire about the origin of the bulbs: By asking, "Did you propagate these bulbs in your nursery from seeds or cuttings?" or "If you obtained these bulbs from a supplier, do you know if the supplier propagated them?" consumers send a message to bulb dealers that conscientious buyers to not wish to participate in the destruction of wild-collected bulbs.

WILDLIFE TRADE IN THE UNITED STATES

The following statistical summary of wildlife imported into the United States is based primarily on 1990–92 reported trade and should be considered minimum. The total annual declared value of all U.S. trade (imports and exports) was roughly $1.2 billion.

Red-lored parrot (*Amazona autumnalis*).
Photo by Steve Cornelius/WWF.

Primates   10,000–12,000 live, mostly for biomedical research

Total declared value: $4–5 million
U.S. health laws do not allow primate imports except for scientific or educational purposes. Most of the primates entering trade are nonendangered species, such as the crab-eating, pigtail, or rhesus macaques, used for biomedical research. Yet some highly endangered monkeys and apes, particularly chimpanzees, are in demand for research needs associated with the AIDS virus and other human diseases. Overall annual imports of primates ranged from 10,000 to 20,000 in the last decade and may be increasing because of growing medical research needs.

Live Birds   100,000–200,000 live, mostly passerine species
Total declared value: $6–7 million
The Wild Bird Conservation Act of 1992 has sharply reduced imports of live birds, especially parrots. At its peak in the mid-1980s, the importation of birds to the United States reached 800,000 animals. Many large parrots, such as hyacinth macaws, caninde macaws, and palm cockatoos, are rare as a result of habitat loss and commercial exploitation. Some bird traders, willing to pay tens of thousands of dollars for protected species, perpetuate the smuggling of rare birds out of countries such as Brazil, Mexico, and Australia. Smuggling

across the U.S.-Mexico border continues to be a major problem and may involve up to 50,000 birds a year, mostly parrots.

Reptiles   1–2 million live
3–4 million whole skins
25–30 million manufactured products
Total declared value: $475–500 million

Trade in crocodilian skins and products, the most valuable of reptile goods in the market, has fluctuated in recent years due to changes in the economy and market for luxury exotic leather goods. More than 85 percent of all imported reptile skins come from Asian snakes and the tegu lizard of South America. Ninety-five percent of all imported reptile skins come from Argentina, Indonesia, Japan, the Philippines, Singapore, Taiwan, Thailand, and Venezuela. Efforts are under way in some countries to establish programs to manage harvest for the skin trade, particularly for certain crocodilians and the tegu lizard. Imports of live reptiles, which involve hundreds of species, increased in the mid-1980s and remain high in the 1990s. There are signs that the live reptile trade is increasing as the live bird trade declines.

Ornamental Fish   200–250 million fish
Total declared value: $50–60 million

Imports include an estimated 300 marine and 300 freshwater species. The majority of imported freshwater fish are captive-bred in fish farms in Southeast Asia, notably Taiwan, Singapore, and Indonesia. With few exceptions, most saltwater (marine) fish are collected from tropical coral reef areas throughout the world. Most wild freshwater fish are imported from Brazil, Colombia, Peru, and Guyana while marine fish are imported primarily from the Philippines and Indonesia.

Mollusks   10–15 million raw shells
45 million manufactured products
Total declared value: $45–50 million

Little is known of the current U.S. trade in mollusk shell and shell products. Most of the overall trade is in shell products from Southeast Asia for the tourist curio market and for sale at U.S. beach resorts. Probably only a small amount of the trade is for the specialized shell collector. With the exception of species such as certain giant clams (*Tridacna spp.*), few mollusk species are protected by national or international laws. The effects on marine ecosystems of unregulated overcollection for the curio trade are not well studied.

Corals	200,000–300,000 colonies or polyps of live corals
	500,000–1 million items of raw coral
	1–2 million products
	Total declared value: $5–6 million

In 1988, the United States prohibited most coral imports from the Philippines, the major coral exporter, because of confusion over that country's national regulations and high levels of illegal trade. Imports have declined slightly since then. Trade in live corals for aquariums was uncommon until the late 1980s when improvements in aquarium technology resulted in steady annual increases in imports. Most imported coral comes from Southeast Asia where ecologically important protected coral reefs are being destroyed for international trade, for locally used building materials, and because of destructive fishing practices, pollution, and siltation.

| Cacti | 3–4 million live plants |

In the late 1970s, the United States imported about 10 million cacti annually. The volume has declined significantly, partly due to more comprehensive CITES enforcement. Much of the trade was from wild-collected cacti in Mexico, although in the late 1980s (using figures based on 1989 trade), stricter regulation and prohibitions reduced imports from Mexico. U.S. nurseries, many of which are located in the Southwest, produce huge numbers of cacti for the domestic market. Nevertheless, many endangered cacti lack either adequate national or international protection.

| Orchids | 2–2.5 million live plants |

The U.S. market for orchids has increased dramatically in the last decade. Improved reporting, as well as actual increased consumer demand, account for the higher number of plants reported in trade. According to figures based on 1989 trade, at least half the current U.S. imports are reported to be artificially propagated.

WILDLIFE TRADE WORLDWIDE

The following figures, which represent estimated minimum annual world trade, are extrapolated from U.S. trade figures or calculated from known world trade figures. The estimated minimum declared value for the wildlife trade worldwide is at least $10 billion annually, excluding timber and fisheries products.

Primates   25,000–30,000 live, mostly for biomedical research

Sampling of animal products traded worldwide. Photo by WWF.

Most of the primates traded around the world are nonendangered species, such as crab-eating macaques, used for biomedical research. Some highly endangered monkeys and apes are still seriously threatened by pet, circus, and biomedical trade demands. For example, private collectors pay large sums of money for protected primates, like the golden-headed tamarin of Brazil or the orangutan from Indonesia. There also remains a limited market for souvenir items, such as hands and skulls from the protected gorilla.

Live Birds   2–5 million live birds

Although perching birds or passerines, such as finches, constitute the greatest number of birds traded internationally, parrots, or psittacines, are perhaps most threatened. In the early 1970s, possibly 7.5 million birds were traded each year. Because of increased restrictions and better enforcement of regulations, the wild bird trade has declined significantly. In recent years, major exporters have been Argentina, Guyana, Indonesia, Senegal, and Tanzania. Many of the large parrots, such as macaws and cockatoos, are rare as a result of habitat loss and commercial exploitation because of high prices paid by some bird traders. This perpetuates the smuggling of these and other rare birds out of countries such as Brazil, Mexico, and Australia. A few of these rare species, such as the Spix's macaw, have been or are being pushed to extinction in the wild because of the pet trade.

Reptiles	3 million live farmed turtles
	2–3 million other live reptiles
	10–15 million raw skins
	50 million manufactured products

Although illegal trade in reptile skins has traditionally been a lucrative business because of the high prices paid for many reptile-leather products in fashion markets, certain crocodilian species are increasingly farmed or ranched for commercial use in a legal and controlled manner. However, illegal trade problems remain with species such as caiman, which are poached in Brazil and smuggled into neighboring countries for illicit export to international markets. Endangered species, like the South American black caiman, are also sometimes killed illegally for their high-quality hides. Products from endangered sea turtles, especially the hawksbill turtle, from the Caribbean and Southeast Asia continue to be of worldwide conservation concern. Recent trade figures indicate that many other species, particularly snakes and lizards, are traded in the hundreds of thousands. Little is known of the effects of such trade, although efforts are under way to develop management programs for some species, such as the tegu lizard in Argentina and Paraguay and certain crocodilians.

Ornamental Fish   500–600 million (freshwater and marine species)

Although at least 95 percent of all freshwater fish entering trade are raised on fish farms, most saltwater species are taken from the sea. Ornamental fish are also being taken from Amazonian tributaries in South America and rift lakes in eastern Africa for the pet trade. Little research has been done to determine the effects, if any, of the removal of these fish from their freshwater ecosystems. In the Philippines, Indonesia, Haiti, and other countries, narcotic drugs or poisonous chemicals, such as cyanide, are sometimes used illegally to stun marine fish for easy capture. In addition to killing the fish by causing permanent damage to vital organs, these toxic chemicals also damage the surrounding coral wildlife and reefs.

Corals   1,000–2,000 tons raw coral

The majority of coral in world trade is fished from tropical coral reefs in the Indo-Pacific and from Southeast Asian countries like Indonesia and the Philippines. In Southeast Asia, protected coral reefs are often illegally mined to provide aquarium decor and coral jewelry to the international market. These reefs are being destroyed from illegal fishing practices such as dynamite fishing and from siltation and pollution. Slow-growing deep water species, such as the black or precious corals, are being excessively fished or dredged to supply consumer markets throughout the world. Tropical coral reefs are important to marine ecosystems because they serve as building blocks for biologically diverse communities, protect the young of commercially valuable marine food species, and serve as natural barriers against beach and island erosion.

Orchids   9–10 million
Of the orchids recorded in international trade in 1989, it is estimated that only 10 percent may be from wild sources. Although most orchids in trade are artificially propagated and traded legally, some illegal trade does exist. Thousands of wild orchids are traded as propagated specimens or are misidentified as unregulated species. In North America, terrestrial orchids, such as the pink ladyslipper, are collected for the horticultural and medicinal markets—often without legal authorization. Other wild orchids, exported illegally from countries like India and Thailand, are improperly labeled as artificially propagated specimens.

Cacti   7–8 million
Most cacti in trade are artificially propagated in Brazil, Japan, the Netherlands, and the United States. An estimated 15 percent of all cactus plants traded annually come from the wild. Wild-collected cacti continue to be smuggled out of Chile, Mexico, and the United States in apparent violation of national laws and CITES. Europe, Japan, and the United States are the major importers of protected cacti.

Appendix A:
CITES Treaty Appendices

A ppendix I
(as of April 1993)

Scientific name   *English common name*

FAUNA   ## ANIMALS

MAMMALIA   ## *MAMMALS*

Marsupialia

Dasyuridae
Sminthopsis longicaudata   Long-tailed dunnart
S. psammophila   Sandhill dunnart

Thylacinidae
* *Thylacinus cynocephalus* p.e.   Thylacine

Peramelidae
* *Chaeropus ecaudatus* p.e.   Pig-footed bandicoot
Perameles bougainville   Western barred bandicoot

Thylacomyidae
Macrotis lagotis   Greater bilby
M. leucura   Lesser bilby

Vombatidae
Lasiorhinus krefftii   Northern hairy-nosed wombat

Scientific name	English common name

Macropodidae
Bettongia spp. — Bettongs
* *Caloprymnus campestris* p.e. — Desert rat-kangaroo
Lagorchestes hirsutus — Rufous hare-wallaby
Lagostrophus fasciatus — Banded hare-wallaby
Onychogalea fraenata — Bridled nailtail wallaby
O. lunata — Crescent nailtail wallaby

Chiroptera

Pteropodidae
Pteropus insularis — Truk flying-fox
P. mariannus — Marianas flying-fox
P. molossinus — Ponape flying-fox
P. phaeocephalus — Mortlock flying-fox
P. pilosus — Large Palau flying-fox
P. samoensis — Samoan flying-fox
P. tonganus — Insular flying-fox

Primates

Lemuridae
Lemuridae spp. — Lemurs, gentle lemurs, sportive lemurs

Cheirogaleidae
Cheirogaleidae spp. — Dwarf lemurs, mouse lemurs, fork-marked lemurs

Indriidae
Indriidae spp. — Indris, sifakas, woolly lemurs

Daubentoniidae
Daubentonia madagascariensis — Aye-aye

Callithricidae
Callithrix jacchus aurita — White-eared marmoset
C.j. flaviceps — Buff-headed marmoset
Leontopithecus spp. — Golden tamarins
Saguinus bicolor — Bare-faced tamarin

Scientific name	English common name
S. leucopus	White-footed tamarin
S. oedipus	Cotton-headed tamarin

Callimiconidae

Callimico goeldii	Goeldi's marmoset

Cebidae

Alouatta palliata	Mantled howler
Ateles geoffroyi frontatus	Black-browed spider monkey
A.g. panamensis	Red spider monkey
Brachyteles arachnoides	Woolly spider monkey
Cacajao spp.	Uakaris
Chiropotes albinasus	White-nosed saki
Lagothrix flavicauda	Yellow-tailed woolly monkey
Saimiri oerstedii	Central American squirrel monkey

Cercopithecidae

Cercocebus galeritus galeritus	Tana River mangabey
Cercopithecus diana	Diana guenon
(includes Cercopithecus roloway)	
Colobus pennantii kirki	Zanzibar red colobus
C. rufomitratus	Tana River colobus
Macaca silenus	Lion-tailed macaque
Nasalis spp.	Pig-tailed langur, proboscis monkey
Papio leucophaeus	Drill
(includes Mandrillus)	
P. sphinx	Mandrill
(includes Mandrillus)	
Presbytis entellus	Hanuman langur
P. geei	Golden langur
P. pileata	Capped langur
P. potenziani	Mentawai langur
Pygathrix spp.	Douc/snub-nosed monkeys
(includes Rhinopethecus)	
Hylobatidae spp.	Gibbons, siamang
Pongidae spp.	Chimpanzees, gorilla, orangutan

Edentata

Dasypodidae

Scientific name	English common name
Priodontes maximus	Giant armadillo

Pholidota

Manidae
Manis temminckii — Temminck's ground pangolin

Lagomorpha

Leporidae
Caprolagus hispidus — Hispid hare
Romerolagus diazi — Volcano rabbit

Rodentia

Sciuridae
Cynomys mexicanus — Mexican prairie dog

Muridae
Leporillus conditor — Greater stick-nest rat
Pseudomys praeconis — Shark bay mouse
Xeromys myoides — False water-rat
Zyzomys pedunculatus — Central rock-rat

Chinchillidae
Chinchilla spp. — Chinchillas
(South American populations)

Cetacea

Platanistidae
Lipotes vexillifer — White flag dolphin
Platanista spp. — Susus

Ziphiidae
Berardius spp. — Fourtooth whales
Hyperoodon spp. — Bottlenose whales

Physeteridae
Physeter macrocephalus — Sperm whale
(includes *Physeter catadon*)

Scientific name	English common name

Delphinidae
Sotalia spp. — Tucuxis
Sousa spp. — Hump-backed dolphins

Phocoenidae
Neophocaena phocaenoides — Finless porpoise
Phocoena sinus — Cochito

Eschrichtidae
Eschrichtius robustus — Gray whale

Balaenopteridae
Balaenoptera acutorostrata — Minke whale
(all populations except Greenland)
B. borealis — Sei whale
B. edeni — Bryde's whale
B. musculus — Blue whale
B. physalus — Fin whale
Megaptera novaeangliae — Humpback whale

Balaenidae
Balaena spp. — Right whales, bowhead whale
Caperea marginata — Pygmy right whale

Carnivora

Canidae
Canis lupus — Grey wolf
(populations of Bhutan, India, Nepal, and Pakistan
Speothos venaticus — Bush dog

Ursidae
Ailuropoda melanoleuca — Giant panda
Helarctos malayanus — Sun bear
Melursus ursinus — Sloth bear
Selenarctos thibetanus — Asiatic black bear
Tremarctos ornatus — Spectacled bear

Scientific name	English common name
Ursus arctos (populations of Bhutan, Mexico, China, and Mongolia)	Brown bear
U. a. isabellinus	Himalayan brown bear

Mustelidae

Aonyx congica (populations of Cameroon and Nigeria)	Cameroon clawless otter
Enhydra lutris nereis	Southern sea otter
Lutra felina	Marine otter
L. longicaudis	South American river otter
L. lutra	Eurasian otter
L. provocax	Southern river otter
Mustela nigripes	Black-footed ferret
Pteronura brasiliensis	Giant otter

Viverridae

Prionodon pardicolor	Spotted linsang

Hyaenidae

Hyaena brunnea	Brown hyaena

Felidae

Acinonyx jubatus (Botswana, Namibia, and Zimbabwe have quotas)	Cheetah
Felis bengalensis bengalensis (all except Chinese population)	Bengal leopard cat
F. caracal (Asian population)	Caracal
F. concolor coryi	Florida puma
F.c. costaricensis	Costa Rican puma
F.c. cougar	Eastern puma
F. geoffroyi	Geoffroy's Cat
F. jacobita	Andean cat
F. marmorata	Marbled cat
F. nigripes	Black-footed cat
F. pardalis	Ocelot
F. pardina	Iberian lynx
F. planiceps	Flat-headed cat

Scientific name	English common name
F. rubiginosa (Indian population)	Rusty-spotted cat
F. temmincki	Asiatic golden cat
F. tigrina oncilla	Costa Rican little spotted cat
F. wiedii nicaraguae	Central American margay
F.w. salvinia	Guatemalan margay
F. tigrina	Little spotted cat
F. wiedii	Margay
F. yagouaroundi (populations of North and Central America)	Jaguarundi
Neofelis nebulosa	Clouded leopard
Panthera leo persica	Asiatic lion
P. onca	Jaguar
P. pardus	Leopard
P. tigris	Tiger
P. uncia	Snow leopard

Pinnipedia

Otariidae

Arctocephalus townsendi	Guadalupe fur seal

Phocidae

Monachus spp.	Monk seals

Proboscidea

Elephantidae

Elephas maximus	Asian elephant
Loxodonta africana	African elephant

Sirenia

Dugongidae

Dugong dugon (except Australian population)	Dugong

Trichechidae

Trichechus inunguis	Amazonian manatee
T. manatus	Caribbean manatee

Scientific name	English common name

Perissodactyla

Equidae

Equus africanus	African wild ass
E. grevyi	Grevy's zebra
E. hemionus hemionus	Mongolian wild ass
E h. khur	Indian wild ass
E. przewalskii	Przewalski's horse
E. zebra zebra	Cape Mountain zebra
Tapiridae spp. (all species not listed on Appendix II)	Tapirs
Rhinocerotidae spp.	Rhinoceroses

Artiodactyla

Suidae

Babyrousa babyrussa	Babirusa
Sus salvanius	Pygmy hog

Tayassuidae

Catagonus wagneri	Chacoan peccary

Camelidae

Vicugna vicugna (except for parts of populations of Chile and Peru)	Vicuña

Cervidae

Blastocerus dichotomus	Marsh deer
Cervus dama mesopotamicus	Persian fallow deer
C. duvauceli	Swamp deer
C. elaphus hanglu	Kashmir red deer
C. eldi	Thamin
C. porcinus annamiticus	Indochinese hog deer
C.p. calamianensis	Calamian hog deer
C.p. kuhli	Kuhl's hog deer
Hippocamelus spp.	Huemuls
Moschus spp. (populations of Afghanistan, Bhutan, Burma,	Musk deer

Scientific name	English common name
India, Nepal, and Pakistan)	
Muntiacus crinifrons	Black muntjac
Ozotoceros bezoarticus	Pampas deer
Pudu pudu	Southern pudu
Bovidae	
Addax nasomaculatus	Addax
Antilocapra americana	Pronghorn
(population of Mexico)	
Bison bison athabascae	Wood bison
Bos gaurus	Gaur
B. mutus	Yak
B. sauveli	Kouprey
Bubalus depressicornis	Lowland anoa
B. mindorensis	Tamarau
B. quarlesi	Mountain anoa
Capra falconeri	Markhor
Capricornis sumatraensis	Mainland serow
Cephalophus jentinki	Jentink's duiker
Gazella dama	Dama gazelle
Hippotragus niger variani	Giant sable antelope
Nemorhaedus goral	Common goral
Oryx dammah	Scimitar-horned oryx
O. leucoryx	Arabian oryx
Ovis ammon hodgsoni	Tibetan argali
O. orientalis ophion	Cyprus mouflon
O. vignei	Urial
Pantholops hodgsoni	Chiru
Rupicapra rupicapra ornata	Abruzzi chamois

AVES

BIRDS

Struthioniformes

Struthionidae

Struthio camelus (populations of
Algeria, Burkina Faso,

Ostrich

Scientific name	English common name

Cameroon, Central African
Republic, Chad, Mali,
Mauritania, Morocco, Niger,
Nigeria, Senegal, and Sudan)

Rheiformes

Rheidae
Pterocnemia pennata   Lesser rhea

Tinamiformes

Tinamidae
Tinamus solitarius   Solitary tinamou

Sphenisciformes

Spheniscidae
Spheniscus humboldti   Humboldt penguin

Podicipediformes

Podicipedidae
Podilymbus gigas   Atitlan grebe

Procellariiformes

Diomedeidae
Diomedea albatrus   Short-tailed albatross

Pelecaniformes

Pelecanidae
Pelecanus crispus   Dalmatian pelican

Sulidae
Papasula abbotti   Abbott's booby

Scientific name	English common name
Fregatidae	
Fregata andrewsi	Christmas Island frigatebird

Ciconiiformes

Ciconiidae	
Ciconia boyciana	Oriental white stork
Jabiru mycteria	Jabiru
Mycteria cinerea	Milky stork
Threskiornithidae	
Geronticus eremita	Northern bald ibis
Nipponia nippon	Japanese crested ibis

Anseriformes

Anatidae	
Anas aucklandica nesiotis	Campbell Island brown teal
A. laysanensis	Laysan duck
A. oustaleti	Marianas duck
Branta canadensis leucopareia	Aleutian goose
B. sandvicensis	Hawaiian goose
Cairina scutulata	White-winged wood duck
* *Rhodonessa caryophyllacea* p.e.	Pink-headed duck

Falconiformes

Cathartidae	
Gymnogyps californianus	California condor
Vultur gryphus	Andean condor
Accipitridae	
Aquila adalberti	
A. heliaca	Imperial eagle
Chondrohierax uncinatus wilsonii	Cuban hook-billed kite
Haliaeetus albicilla	White-tailed eagle
H. leucocephalus	Bald eagle
Harpia harpyja	South American harpy eagle
Pithecophaga jefferyi	Philippine eagle

Scientific name	English common name

Falconidae
Falco araea	Seychelles kestrel
F. jugger	Laggar falcon
F. newtoni aldabranus	Aldabra kestrel
F. pelegrinoides	
F. peregrinus	Peregrine falcon
F. punctatus	Mauritius kestrel
F. rusticolus	Gyr falcon

Galliformes

Megapodiidae
Macrocephalon maleo	Maleo

Cracidae
Crax blumenbachii	Red-billed curassow
Mitu mitu mitu	Greater razor-billed curassow
Oreophasis derbianus	Horned guan
Penelope albipennis	White-winged guan
Pipile jacutinga	Black-fronted piping guan
Pipile pipile pipile	Trinidad piping guan

Phasianidae
Catreus wallichii	Cheer pheasant
Colinus virginianus ridgwayi	Masked bobwhite
Crossoptilon crossoptilon	White-eared pheasant
C. harmani	
C. mantchuricum	Brown-eared pheasant
Lophophorus spp.	Monals
Lophura edwardsi	Edwards' pheasant
L. imperialis	Imperial pheasant
L. swinhoii	Swinhoe's pheasant
Polyplectron emphanum	Palawan peacock-pheasant
Rheinardia ocellata	Crested argus pheasant
Syrmaticus ellioti	Elliot's pheasant
S. humiae	Hume's pheasant
S. mikado	Mikado pheasant
Tetraogallus caspius	Caspian snowcock

Scientific name	English common name
T. tibetanus	Tibetan snowcock
Tragopan blythii	Blyth's tragopan
T. caboti	Cabot's tragopan
T. melanocephalus	Western tragopan
Tympanuchus cupido attwateri	Attwater's prairie chicken

Gruiformes

Gruidae
Grus americana	Whooping crane
G. canadensis nesiotes	Cuban sandhill crane
G.c. pulla	Mississippi sandhill crane
G. japonensis	Red-crowned crane
G. leucogeranus	Siberian crane
G. monacha	Hooded crane
G. nigricollis	Black-necked crane
G. vipio	White-naped crane

Rallidae
Gallirallus sylvestris	Lord Howe wood rail

Rhynochetidae
Rhynochetus jubata	Kagu

Otididae
Ardeotis nigriceps	Great Indian bustard
Chlamydotis undulata	Houbara bustard
Eupodotis bengalensis	Bengal florican

Charadriiformes

Scolopacidae
Numenius borealis	Eskimo curlew
N. tenuirostris	Slender-billed curlew
Tringa guttifer	Nordmann's greenshank

Laridae
Larus relictus	Relict gull

Scientific name	English common name

Columbiformes

Columbidae
Caloenas nicobarica	Nicobar pigeon
Ducula mindorensis	Mindoro imperial pigeon

Psittachiformes

Psittacidae
Amazona arausiaca	Red-necked amazon
A. *barbadensis*	Yellow-shouldered amazon
A. *brasiliensis*	Red-tailed amazon
A. *guildingii*	St. Vincent amazon
A. *imperialis*	Imperial amazon
A. *leucocephala*	Cuban amazon
A. *pretrei*	Red-spectacled amazon
A. *rhodocorytha*	Red-crowned amazon
A. *tucumana*	Tucuman amazon
A. *versicolor*	St. Lucia amazon
A. *vinacea*	Vinaceous amazon
A. *vittata*	Puerto Rican amazon
Anodorhynchus spp.	Blue macaws
Ara ambigua	Buffon's macaw
A. *glaucogularis*	Blue-throated macaw
A. *macao*	Scarlet macaw
A. *maracana*	Illiger's macaw
A. *militaris*	Military macaw
A. *rubrogenys*	Red-fronted macaw
Aratinga guarouba	Golden conure
Cacatua goffini	Goffin's cockatoo
C. *haematuropygia*	Red-vented cockatoo
C. *moluccensis*	Salmon-crested cockatoo
Cyanopsitta spixii	Spix's macaw
Cyanoramphus auriceps forbesi	Forbes' yellow-fronted parakeet
C. *cookii*	Norfolk parrot
C. *novaezelandiae*	Red-fronted parakeet
Cyclopsitta diophthalma coxeni	Coxen's double-eyed fig parrot
Neophema chrysogaster	Orange-bellied parrot

Scientific name	English common name
Ognorhynchus icterotis	Yellow-eared conure
* Pezoporus occidentalis p.e.	Night parrot
P. wallicus	Ground parrot
Pionopsitta pileata	Brazilian pileated parrot
Proesciger aterrimus	Palm cockatoo
Psephotus chrysopterygius	
P. dissimilis	Golden-shouldered parrot
* P. pulcherrimus p.e.	Paradise parrot
Psittacula echo	Mauritius parakeet
Psittacus erithacus princeps	Principe grey parrot
Pyrrhura cruentata	Blue-throated conure
Rhynchopsitta spp.	Thick-billed parrots
Strigops habroptilus	Kakapo

Strigiformes

Tytonidae
Tyto soumagnei Madagascar owl

Strigidae
Athene blewitti	Forest owlet
Mimizuki gurneyi	Mindanao owl
Ninox novaeseelandiae undulata	Norfolk Island boobook owl
N. squamipila natalis	Christmas Island boobook owl

Apodiformes

Trochilidae
Glaucis dohrnii Hook-billed hermit

Trogoniformes

Trogonidae
Pharomachrus mocinno Resplendent quetzal

Scientific name	English common name

Coraciiformes

Bucerotidae

Aceros nipalensis	Rufous-necked hornbill
A. subruficollis	Plain pouched hornbill
Buceros bicornis	Great Indian hornbill
B. (Rhinoplax) vigil	Helmeted hornbill

Piciformes

Picidae

Campephilus imperialis	Imperial woodpecker
Dryocopus javensis richardsi	Tristram's white-bellied woodpecker

Passeriformes

Cotingidae

Cotinga maculata	Banded cotinga
Xipholena atropurpurea	White-winged cotinga

Pittidae

P. gurneyi	Gurney's Pitta
Pitta kochi	Whiskered pitta

Atrichornithidae

Atrichornis clamosus	Noisy scrub-bird

Hirundinidae

Pseudochelidon sirintarae	White-eyed river martin

Muscicapidae

* *Dasyornis broadbenti litoralis* p.e.	Western rufous bristlebird
D. longirostris	Western bristlebird
Picathartes spp.	Picathartes

Zosteropidae

Zosterops albogularis	White-chested white-eye

Scientific name	English common name

Meliphagidae
Lichenostomus melanops cassidix Helmeted honeyeater

Fringillidae
Carduelis cucullata Red siskin

Sturnidae
Leucopsar rothschildi Rothschild's myna

REPTILIA

REPTILES

Testudinata

Emydidae
Batagur baska Common batagur
Clemmys muhlenbergi Bog turtle
Geoclemys hamiltonii Black pond turtle
Kachuga tecta tecta Indian tent turtle
Melanochelys tricarinata Three-keeled land turtle
Morenia ocellata Burmese swamp turtle
Terrapene coahuila Aquatic box turtle

Testudinidae
Geochelone elephantopus Galapagos giant tortoise
G. radiata Radiated tortoise
G. yniphora Madagascar tortoise
Gopherus flavomarginatus Bolson tortoise
Psammobates geometricus Geometric tortoise
Cheloniidae spp. Marine turtles

Dermochelyidae
Dermochelys coriacea Leatherback turtle

Trionychidae
Lissemys punctata punctata Indian flap-shell turtle
Trionyx ater Black soft-shell turtle
T. gangeticus Ganges soft-shell turtle
T. hurum Peacock-marked soft-shell turtle
T. nigricans Dark soft-shell turtle

Scientific name	English common name

Chelidae
Pseudemydura umbrina Short-necked turtle

Crocodylia

Alligatoridae
Alligator sinensis Chinese alligator
Caiman crocodilus apaporiensis Rio Apaporis spectacled caiman
C. latirostris Broad-nosed caiman
Melanosuchus niger Black caiman

Crocodylidae
Crocodylus acutus American crocodile
C. cataphractus Sharp-nosed crocodile
C. intermedius Orinoco crocodile
C. moreletii Morelet's crocodile
C. niloticus Nile crocodile
(Except populations of Botswana, Ethiopia,
Kenya, Malawi, Mozambique, United
Republic of Tanzania, Zambia, and Zimbabwe
and populations of the following countries,
which are subject to export quotas: Madagascar,
Somalia, South Africa, and Uganda))
C. novaeguineae mindorensis Mindoro crocodile
C. palustris Mugger crocodile
C. porosus Estuarine crocodile
(Except populations of Australia and
Papua New Guinea and populations of
Indosnesia, which is subject to an export quota)
C. rhombifer Cuban crocodile
C. siamensis Siamese crocodile
Osteolaemus tetraspis West African dwarf crocodile
Tomistoma schlegelii False gharial

Gavialidae
Gavialis gangeticus Gharial

Scientific name	English common name

Rhynchocephalia

Sphenodontidae
Sphenodon punctatus — Tuatara

Sauria

Iguanidae
Brachylophus spp. — Fiji iguanas
Cyclura spp. — West Indian rock iguanas
Sauromalus varius — San Esteban Island chuckwalla

Lacertidae
Gallotia simonyi — Hierro giant lizard

Varanidae
Varanus bengalensis — Bengal monitor
V. flavescens — Yellow monitor
V. griseus — Desert monitor
V. komodoensis — Komodo dragon

Serpentes

Boidae
Acrantophis spp. — Madagascar boas
Boa constrictor occidentalis — Argentine boa constrictor
Bolyeria multocarinata — Round Island boa
Casarea dussumieri — Keel-scaled boa
Epicrates inornatus — Puerto Rican boa
E. monensis — Mona Island boa
E. subflavus — Jamaican boa
Python molurus molurus — Indian rock python
Sanzinia madagascariensis — Madagascar tree boa

Viperidae
Vipera ursinii (population of Ursini's viper Europe, excluding the area which formerly constituted the Soviet Union)

Scientific name	English common name

AMPHIBIA

Caudata

Cryptobranchidae
Andrias spp. — Giant salamanders

Anura

Bufonidae
Atelopus varius zeteki — Golden frog
Bufo superciliaris — Cameroon toad
Nectophrynoides spp. — Viviparous African toads

Microhylidae
Dyscophus antongilii — Tomato frog

PISCES

Acipenserifprmes

Acipenseridae
Acipenser brevirostrum — Shortnose sturgeon
A. sturio — Common sturgeon

Coelacahthiformes

Coelacanthidae
Latimeria chalumnae — Coelacanth

Osteoglossiformes

Osteoglossidae
Scleropages formosus — Asian bony-tongue
  (population of Indonesia)

AMPHIBIANS

FISH

Scientific name	*English common name*

Cypriniformes

Cyprinidae
Probarbus jullieni   Ikan temoleh

Catostomidae
Chasmistes cujus   Cui ui

Siluriformes

Schilbeidae
Pangasianodon gigas   Giant catfish

Perciformes

Sciaenidae
Cynoscion macdonaldi   Totoaba

INSECTA   *INSECTS*

Lepidoptera

Papilionidae
Ornithoptera alexandrae   Queen Alexandra's birdwing
Papilio chikae   Luzon swallowtail
P. homerus   Homerus swallowtail
P. hospiton   Corsican swallowtail

MOLLUSCA   *MOLLUSKS*

Uhionoia

Unionidae
Conradilla caelata   Birdwing pearly mussel
Dromus dromas   Dromedary pearly mussel
Epioblasma curtisi   Curtis' pearly mussel

Scientific name	English common name
E. florentina	Yellow-blossom pearly mussel
E. sampsoni	Sampson's pearly mussel
E. sulcata perobliqua	White catspaw mussel
E. torulosa gubernaculum	Green-blossom pearly mussel
E.t. torulosa	Tubercled-blossom pearly mussel
E. turgidula	Turgid-blossom pearly mussel
E. walkeri	Brown-blossom pearly mussel
Fusconaia cuneolus	Fine-rayed pigtoe pearly mussel
F. edgariana	Shiny pigtoe pearly mussel
Lampsilis higginsi	Higgins' eye pearly mussel
L. orbiculata orbiculata	Pinck mucket pearly mussel
L. satura	Plain pocketbook pearly mussel
L. virescens	Alabama lamp pearly mussel
Plethobasus cicatricosus	White warty-back pearly mussel
P. cooperianus	Orange-footed pimpleback mussel
Pleurobema plenum	Rough pigtoe pearly mussel
Potamilus capax	Fat pocketbook pearly mussel
Quadrula intermedia	Cumberland monkey-face pearly mussel
Q. sparsa	Appalachian monkey-face pearly mussel
Toxolasma cylindrella	Pale lilliput pearly mussel
Unio nickliniana	Nicklin's pearly mussel
U. tampicoensis tecomatensis	Tampico pearly mussel
Villosa trabalis	Cumberland bean pearly mussel

Stylommatophora

Achatinellidae
Achatinella spp.   Oahu tree snails

FLORA   # PLANTS

Agavaceae
Agave arizonica   New River agave
A. parviflora   Little princess agave
Nolina interrata   Dehesa beargrass

Apocynacceae
Pachypodium baronii   Elephant's trunks

Scientific name	English common name
P. brevicaule	
P. decaryi	
P. namaquanum	

Araucariaceae

| *Araucaria araucana* | Monkey-puzzle tree |
| (population of Chile) | |

Cactaceae

Ariocarpus spp.	Living-rock cactus
Astrophytum asterias	Star cactus
Aztekium ritteri	Aztec cactus
Coryphantha minima	Nellie's cory cactus
C. sneedii	Sneed's pincushion cactus
C. werdermanii	Jabali pincushion cactus
Discocactus spp.	
Echinocereus ferreirianus var.	Lindsay's cactus
lindsayi	
E. schmollii	Lamb's-tail cactus
Leuchtenbergia principis	Agave cactus
Mammillaria pectinifera	
M. plumosa	Feather cactus
M. solisioides	
Melocactus conoideus	
M. deinacanthus	
M. glaucescens	
M. paucispinus	
Obregonia denegrii	Artichoke cactus
Pachycereus militaris	Teddy-bear cactus
Pediocactus bradyi	Brady's pincushion cactus
P. despainii	Despain's cactus
P. knowltonii	Knowlton's cactus
P. papyracanthus	Grama-grass cactus
P. paradinei	Paradine's cactus
P. peeblesianus	Peebles' Navajo cactus
P. sileri	Siler's pincushion cactus
P. winkleri	Winkler's cactus

Scientific name	English common name
Pelecyphora spp.	Hatchet cactus, pine-cone cactus
Sclerocactus brevihamaticus	Tobusch's fishhook cactus
S. glaucus	Uinta Basin hookless cactus
S. erectocentrus	Needle-spined pineapple cactus
S. mariposensis	Mariposa cactus
S. mesae-verdae	Mesa Verde cactus
S. pubispinus	Great Basin fishhook cactus
S. wrightiae	Wright's fishhook cactus
Strombocactus disciformis	Disk cactus
Turbinicarpus spp.	Turbinicacti
Uebelmannia spp.	

Compositae
Saussurea costus   Kuth

Crassulaceae

Dudleya stolonifera	Laguna Beach dudleya
D. traskiae	Santa Barbara Island dudleya

Cupressaceae

Fitzroya cupressoides   Alerce
Pilgerodendron uviferum

Cycadaceae
Cycas beddomei   Beddomes's cycad

Euphorbiaceae
(includes natural   Euphorbias
hybrids)
Euphorbia ambovombensis
E. cylindrifolia
E. decaryi
E. francoisii
E. moratii
E. parvicyathophora
E. primulifolia
E. quartziticola
E. tulearensis

Scientific name	English common name
Fouquieriaceae	
Fouquieria fasciculata	
F. purpusii	
Leguminosae	
Dalbergia nigra	Brazilian rosewood
Liliaceae	
Aloe albida	
A. pillansii	
A. polyphylla	Spiral aloe
A. thorncroftii	
A. vossii	
Nepenthaceae	
Nepenthes khasiana	Indian pitcher-plant
N. rajah	Kanabalu pitcher-plant
Orchidaceae	
+*Cattleya skinneri*	White nun orchid
+*C. trianae*	Christmas orchid
+*Didiciea cunninghamii*	
+*Laelia jongheana*	
+*L. lobata*	
+*Lycaste skinneri var. alba*	
+*Paphiopedilum* spp.	Lady's slipper orchids
+*Peristeria elata*	Holy ghost orchid
+*Phragmipedium* spp.	Slipper orchids
+*Renanthera imschootiana*	Red vanda orchid
+*Vanda coerulea*	Blue vanda orchid
Pinaceae	
Abies guatemalensis	Guatemalan fir
Podocarpaceae	
Podocarpus parlatorei	Parlatore's podocarp

Scientific name	English common name

Proteaceae
Orothamnus zeyheri   Marsh rose protea
Protea odorata

Rubiaceae
Balmea stormiae   Ayuque

Sarraceniaceae
Sarracenia alabamensis spp.   Alabama canebrake pitcher-plant
S. jonesii   Mountain sweet pitcher-plant
S. oreophila   Green pitcher-plant

Stangeriaceae
Stangeria eriopus   Hottentot's head

Zamiaceae
Ceratozamia spp.
Chigua spp.   Cycads
Encephalartos spp.   Bread-palms
Microcycas calocoma   Palma corcho

---

* Possibly extinct.
+ Tissues, cultures and flasked seedling cultures are not subject to the provisions of CITES.

A

ppendix II
(as of April 1993)

Scientific name	English common name
FAUNA	**ANIMALS**
MAMMALIA	*MAMMALS*

Monotremata

Tachyglossidae
Zaglossus spp.   Long-beaked echidnas

Marsupialia

Phalangeridae
Phalanger maculatus   Common spotted cuscus
P. orientalis   Grey cuscus

Burramyidae
Burramys parvus   Mountain pygmy-possum

Macropodidae
Dendrolagus bennettianus   Bennett's tree-kangaroo
D. inustus   Grizzled tree-kangaroo
D. lumholtzi   Lumholtz' tree-kangaroo
D. ursinus   Vogelkop tree-kangaroo

Chiroptera

Pteropodidae
Acerodon spp.   Flying-foxes
Pteropus spp.   Fruit bats
 (Species not listed on
 Appendix I)

Scientific name	English common name

Primates

All nonhuman primates not listed on Appendix I (includes family Tupaiidae) · Primates

Edentata

Myrmecophagidae
Myrmecophaga tridactyla · Giant anteater

Bradypodidae
Bradypus variegatus · Brown-throated sloth

Pholidota

Manidae
Manis crassicaudata · Indian pangolin
M. javanica · Malayan pangolin
M. pentadactyla · Chinese pangolin

Rodentia

Sciuridae
Ratufa spp. · Oriental giant squirrels

Cetacea

All cetacean species and populations not listed on Appendix I

Carnivora

Canidae
† *Canis lupus* (populations of Bhutan, India, Nepal, and Pakistan) · Grey wolf

Scientific name	English common name
Chrysocyon brachyurus	Maned wolf
Cuon alpinus	Dhole
Dusicyon culpaeus	Colpeo fox
D. griseus	Argentine grey fox
D. gymnocercus	Pampas fox
D. thous	Crab-eating fox
Vulpes cana	Blanford's fox
V. zerda	Fennec fox

Ursidae

Ursus americanus	Black bear
† *U. arctos* (except subspecies listed on Appendix I)	Brown bear
U. maritimus	Polar bear

Procyonidae

Ailurus fulgens	Lesser panda

Mustelidae

Conepatus humboldtii	Patagonian hog-nosed skunk
Lutrinae spp. (species not listed on Appendix I)	Otters

Viverridae

Cryptoprocta ferox	Fossa
Cynogale bennettii	Otter-civet
Eupleres goudotii	Falanouc
Fossa fossa	Malagasy civet
Hemigalus derbyanus	Banded palm civet
Prionodon linsang	Banded linsang
Felidae spp. (all species and populations not listed on Appendix I)	Cats

Scientific name	English common name

Pinnipedia

Otariidae
Arctocephalus spp. (all species   Fur seals
  not listed on Appendix I)

Phocidae
Mirounga leonina   Southern elephant-seal

Sirenia

Dugongidae
† *Dugong dugon*   Dugong
  (Australian population)

Trichechidae
Trichechus senegalensis   African manatee

Perissodactyla

Equidae
Equus hemionus (subspecies not   Asiatic wild ass
  listed on Appendix I)
E. zebra hartmannae   Hartmann's mountain zebra

Tapiridae
Tapirus terrestris   Brazilian tapir

Artiodactyla

Tayassuidae spp. (all species   Peccaries
  not listed on Appendix I,
  except U.S. populations)

Hippopotamidae
Choeropsis liberiensis   Pygmy hippopotamus

Scientific name	English common name

Camelidae
Lama guanicoe — Guanaco
† *Vicugna vicugna* (parts of populations of Chile and Peru) — Vicuña

Cervidae
Cervus elaphus bactrianus — Bactrian red deer
Moschus spp. (populations not listed on Appendix I) — Musk deer
Pudu mephistophiles — Northern pudu

Bovidae
Ammotragus lervia — Barbary sheep
Budorcas taxicolor — Takin
Cephalophus dorsalis — Bay duiker
C. monticola — Blue duiker
C. ogilbyi — Ogilby's duiker
C. sylvicultor — Yellow-backed duiker
C. zebra — Banded duiker
Damaliscus dorcas dorcas — Bontebok
Kobus leche — Lechwe
† *Ovis ammon* (except for subspecies listed on Appendix I) — Argali
† *O. canadensis* (population of Mexico) — Bighorn

AVES

BIRDS

Rheiformes

Rheidae
Rhea americana — Greater rhea

Scientific name	English common name

Tinamiformes

Tinamidae
Rhynchotus rufescens maculicollis	Bolivian rufous tinamou
R.r. pallescens	Argentine rufous tinamou
R.r. rufescens	Brazilian rufous tinamou

Sphenisciformes

Spheniscidae
Spheniscus demersus	Jackass penguin

Ciconiiformes
Balaenicipitidae
Balaeniceps rex	Shoebill

Ciconiidae
Ciconia nigra	Black stork

Threskiornithidae
Eudocimus ruber	Scarlet ibis
Geronticus calvus	Southern bald ibis
Platalea leucorodia	White spoonbill
Phoenicopteridae spp.	Flamingos

Anseriformes

Anatidae
Anas aucklandica aucklandica	Auckland Island brown teal
A. bernieri	Madagascar teal
A. formosa	Baikal teal
A.a. chlorotis	New Zealand brown teal
Branta ruficollis	Red-breasted goose
Coscoroba coscoroba	Coscoroba swan
Cygnus melanocorypha	Black-necked swan
Dendrocygna arborea	West Indian whistling duck
Oxyura leucocephala	White-headed duck
Sarkidiornis melanotos	Comb duck

Scientific name	English common name

Falconiformes

Falconiformes spp.   All birds of prey
  (Not listed on Appendix I,
  except *Cathartidae* spp.)   New World vultures

Galliformes

Phasianidae
Argusianus argus   Great argus pheasant
Gallus sonneratii   Grey junglefowl
Ithaginis cruentus   Blood pheasant
Pavo muticus   Green peafowl
Polyplectron bicalcaratum   Grey peacock-pheasant
P. germaini   Germain's peacock-pheasant
P. malacense   Malaysian peacock-pheasant
P. schleiermacheri   Borean peacock-pheasant

Gruiformes

Turnicidae
Turnix melanogaster   Black-breasted buttonquail

Pedionomidae
Pedionomus torquatus   Plains-wanderer

Gruidae spp. (all species not   Cranes
  listed on Appendix I)

Rallidae
Gallirallus australis hectori   Buff weka

Otididae spp. (all species not   Bustards
  listed on Appendix I)

Colunbiformes

Columbidae
Gallicolumba luzonica   Luzon bleeding-heart dove

Scientific name	English common name
Goura spp.	Crowned pigeons

Psittaciformes

Psittaciformes spp. (All species not listed on Appendix I, except;	Parrots, lories, macaws, parrakets, etc.
Melopsittacus undulatus	Budgerigar
Nymphicus hollandicus	Cockatiel
and *Psittacula krameri*)	Rose-ringed parakeet

Cuculiformes

Musophagidae

Tauraco corythaix	Knysna turaco
T. fischeri	Fischer's turaco
T. livingstonii	Livingstone's turaco
T. persa	Guinea turaco
T. porphyreolophus	Purple-crested turaco
Musophaga porphyreolophus	
T. schalowi	Schalow's turaco
T. schuetti	Black-billed turaco

Strigiformes

All owl species not listed on Appendix I

Apodiformes

Trochilidae spp. (all species not listed on Appendix I)	Hummingbirds

Coraciformes

Bucerotidae

Aceros spp. (all species not listed on Appendix I)	Hornbills

Scientific name	English common name
Anorrhinus spp.	Hornbills
Anthracoceros spp.	Hornbills
Buceros spp. (all subspecies not listed on Appendix I)	
Penelopides spp.	Hornbills
Ptilolaemus spp.	Hornbills

Piciformes

Ramphastidae
Pteroglossus aracari	Toucans
P. viridis	
Ramphastos sulfuratus	Toucans
R. toco	
R. tucanus	
R. vitellinus	

Passeriformes

Cotingidae
Rupicola spp.	Cocks-of-the-rock

Pittidae
Pitta nympha	Fairy pitta
P. guajana	Banded pitta

Muscicapidae
Cyornis ruckii	Rueck's blue flycatcher

Emberizidae
Gubernatrix cristata	Yellow cardinal
Paroaria capitata	Yellow-billed cardinal
P. coronata	Red-crested cardinal

Fringillidae
Carduelis yarrellii	Yellow-faced siskin

Estrildidae
Poephila cincta cincta	Southern black-throated finch

Scientific name	English common name
Paradisaeidae spp.	Birds of paradise

REPTILIA

Testudinata

Dermatemydidae
Dermatemys mawii

Emydidae
Clemmys insculpta

Testudinidae spp. (all species
and subspecies not listed on
Appendix I)

Pelomedusidae
Erymnochelys madagascariensis
Peltocephalus dumeriliana
Podocnemis spp.

Crocodylia

All crocodile spp. not listed
on Appendix I except those subject
to specific annual export
quotas for some species and
countries

Sauria

Gekkonidae
Cyrtodactylus serpensinsula
Phelsuma spp.

Agamidae
Uromastyx spp.

REPTILES

Central American river turtle

Wood turtle

Tortoises

Madagascar sideneck turtle
Parrot-beaked turtle
South American river turtles

Serpent Island gecko
Day geckos

Spiny-tailed lizards

Scientific name	English common name
Chamaeleonidae	
Bradypodion spp.	Dwarf chameleons
Chamaeleo spp.	Chameleons
Iguanidae	
Amblyrhynchus cristatus	Galapagos marine iguana
Conolophus spp.	Galapagos land iguanas
Iguana spp.	Green iguanas
Phrynosoma coronatum	San Diego horned lizard
Lacertidae	
Podarcis lilfordi	Lilford's wall lizard
P. pityusensis	Ibiza wall lizard
Cordylidae	
Cordylus spp.	Girdled lizards
Pseudocordylus spp.	Crag lizards
Teiidae	
Cnemidophorus hyperythrus	Orange-throated whiptail
Crocodilurus lacertinus	Dragon lizard
Dracaena spp.	Caiman lizards
Tupinambis spp.	Tegus
Scincidae	
Corucia zebrata	Prehensile-tailed skink
Xenosauridae	
Shinisaurus crocodilurus	Chinese crocodile lizard
Helodermatidae	
Heloderma spp.	Gila monster, beaded lizard
Varanidae	
† *Varanus* spp. (all species not listed on Appendix I)	Monitors

Scientific name	English common name

Serpentes

Boidae spp. (all species not
listed on Appendix I)   Boas and pythons

Colubridae
Clelia clelia   Mussurana
Cyclagras gigas   False cobra
Elachistodon westermanni   Indian egg-eating snake
Ptyas mucosus   Oriental rat snake

Elapidae
Hoplocephalus bungaroides   Broad-headed snake
Naja naja   Asiatic cobra
Ophiophagus hannah   King cobra

Viperidae
Vipera wagneri   Wagner's viper

AMPHIBIA   ## *AMPHIBIANS*

Caudata

Ambystomidae
Ambystoma dumerilii   Achoque
A. mexicanum   Axolotl

Anura

Bufonidae
Bufo retiformis   Sonoran green toad

Myobatrachidae
Rheobatrachus spp.   Platypus frog/gastric-brooding frog
Dendrobatidae
Dendrobates spp.   Poison-arrow frogs
Phyllobates spp.   Poison-arrow frogs

Scientific name	English common name

Ranidae
Rana hexadactyla — Six-fingered frog
R. tigerina — Indian bullfrog

PISCES — *FISH*

Ceratodiformes

Ceratodidae
Neoceratodus forsteri — Australian lungfish

Acipenseriformes

Acipenseridae
Acipenser oxyrhynchus — Atlantic sturgeon

Polyodontidae
Polyodon spathula — Paddlefish

Osteoglossiformes

Osteoglossidae
Arapaima gigas — Pirarucu
Scleropages formosus
(population of Indonesia subject
to export quotas)

Cypriniformes

Cyprinidae
Caecobarbus geertsi — African blind barb fish

Scientific name	English common name

INSECTA   *INSECTS*

Lepidoptera

Papilionidae

Bhutanitis spp.	Bhutanitis swallowtails
Ornithoptera spp. (all species not listed on Appendix I)	Birdwing butterflies
Parnassius apollo	Mountain apolloy
Teinopalpus spp.	Kaiser-I-Hinds
Trogonoptera spp.	Birdwing butterflies
Troides spp.	Birdwing butterflies

ARACHNIDA   *ARACHNIDS*

Araneae

Theraphosidae

Brachypelma smithi	Mexican red-kneed tarantula

ANNELIDA   *ANNELIDS*

Arhynchobdellae

Hirudinidae

Hirudo medicinalis	Medicinal leech

MOLLUSCA   *MOLLUSKS*

Veneroida

Tridacnidae spp.	Giant clams

Scientific name	English common name

Unionoida

Unionidae
Cyprogenia aberti	Edible pearly mussel
Epioblasma torulosa rangiana	Tan-blossom pearly mussel
Fusconaia subrotunda	Long solid mussel
Lampsilis brevicula	Ozark lamp pearly mussel
Lexingtonia dolabelloides	Slab-sided pearly mussel
Pleurobema clava	Club pearly mussel

Stylomatophora

Camaenidae
Papustyla pulcherrima	Manus green tree snail

Paryphantidae	
Paryphanta spp.	Amber snails
(all New Zealand species)	

Mesogatropoda

Strombidae
Strombus gigas	Queen conch
Anthozoa	Anthozoans
**Antipatharia* spp.	Black corals
**Scleractinia* spp.	Stoney corals
**Pocilloporidae*	
**Pocillopora* spp.	Brown stem cluster corals
**Seriatopora* spp.	Bird's nest corals
**Stylophora* spp.	Cauliflower corals
Acroporidae	
**Acropora* spp.	Branch corals

Scientific name	English common name
**Agariciidae	
**Pavona spp.	Cactus corals
_Fungiidae	
**Fungia spp.	Mushroom corals
**Halomitra spp.	Bowl corals
**Polyphyllia spp.	Feather corals
**Faviidae	
**Favia spp.	Brain corals
**Platygyra spp.	Brain corals
**Merulinidae	
**Merulina spp.	Merulina corals
**Mussidae	
**Lobophyllia spp.	Brain root corals
**Pectiniidae	
**Pectinia spp.	Lettuce corals
**Caryophylliidae	
**Euphyllia spp.	Brain trumpet corals

HYDROZOA   HYDROZOANS

Athecata

**Milleporidae spp.	Wello fire corals
**Stylasteridae spp.	Scarlet corals

ALCYONARIA   ALCYONARIANS

**Coenothecalia spp.

Scientific name	English common name

**Helioporidae
**Heliopora spp.   Blue corals

Stolonifera

**Tubiporidae
**Tubipora spp.   Organpipe corals

FLORA   # PLANTS

Agavaceae
Agave victoriae-reginae   Queen agave

Amaryllidaceae
Galanthus spp.   Snowdrops
 (including natural hybrids)
Sternbergia spp.   Winter daffodil

Apocynaceae
❖Pachypodium spp.   Elephant's trunks
 (except for Appendix I species)

Rauvolfia serpentina   Rauvolfia
 (except chemical derivatives)

Araceae
Alocasia sanderiana

Araliaceae
Panax quinquefolius   American ginseng

Araucariaceae
Araucaria araucana   Monkey-puzzle tree
 (except Chilean population)

Asclepiadaceae
Ceropegia spp.   Rosary vines
Frerea indica

Scientific name	English common name

Berberidaceae
❖❖*Podophyllum hexandrum*

Bromeliaceae

Tillandsia harisii	Air plants
T. *kammii*	
T. *kautskyi*	
T. *mauryana*	
T. *sprengeliana*	
T. *sucrei*	
T. *xerographica*	

Byblidaceae

Byblis spp.	Byblises

Cactaceae
(all species not listed on
Appendix I)

Caryocaraceae
✛*Caryocar costaricense*

Cephalotaceae

Cephalotus follicularis	Albany pitcherplant
Cyatheaceae spp.	Tree ferns

Cycadaceae spp.

(all species	Cycads
not listed on Appendix I)	

Diapensiaceae

Shortia galacifolia	Oconee-bells
Dicksoniaceae spp.	Tree ferns

Scientific name	English common name

Didiereaceae spp.

Dioscoreaceae
Dioscorea deltoidea

Droseraceae
Dionaea muscipula   Venus flytrap

Ericaceae
Kalmia cuneata   White wicky

Euphorbiaceae
Euphorbia spp. (all species not   Euphorbes
listed on Appendix I)

Fouquieriaceae
Fouquieria columnaris   Boojum tree

Juglandaceae
✤*Oreomunnea* (=*Engelhardtia*) *pterocarpa*

Leguguminosae
✤*Pericopsis elata*   Afrormosia
❖*Platymiscium pleiostachyum*   Macawood

Liliaceae
☉*Aloe* spp. (all species not   Aloes
listed on Appendix I)

Meliaceae
✤*Swietenia humilis*   Mexican mahogany
✤*S. mahagoni*   Caribbean mahogany

Nepenthaceae
Nepenthes spp. (all species   Asian pitcher-plants
not listed on Appendix I)

Orchidaceae   Orchids
(all species not listed on Appendix I)

Scientific name	English common name

Palmae
Chrysalidocarpus decipiens — Palm
Neodypsis decaryi — Palm

Podophyllaceae
Podophyllum hexandrum (except chemical derivatives) — Himalayan Mayapple

Portulacaceae
Anacampseros spp.
Lewisia cotyledon — Siskiyou lewisia
L. maguirei — Maguire's lewisia
L. serrata — Saw-toothed lewisia
L. tweedyi — Tweedy's lewisia

Primulaceae
Cyclamen spp. — Cyclamens

Sarraceniaceae
Darlingtonia californica — California pitcher-plant
Sarracenia spp. (all species not listed on Appendix I) — North American pitcher-plants

Theaceae
Camellia chrysantha — Jinhuacha

Welwitschiaceae
Welwitschia mirabilis — Welwitschia

*Zamiaceae — Zamias
(all species not listed on Appendix I)

Zingiberaceae
Hedychium philippinense

Zygophyillaceae
✠Guaiacum officinale
✠G. sanctum — Tree of life

+   Dead specimens only.

†   Specific populations, subspecies, or species.

** Excluding fossils.

*   Not including seeds.

✚ Designates saw-logs, sawn timber, and veneers.

❖ Designates everything except seeds, spores, pollen, tissue cultures, and flasked seedling cultures.

❖❖ Designates all parts except seeds, pollen, tissue cultures, flasked seedling cultures, and chemical derivatives.

Ⓐ Designates all parts except seeds, pollen, tissue cultures, flasked seedling cultures, and separate leaves of artificially propogated plants.

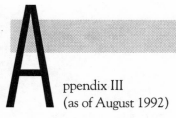

ppendix III
(as of August 1992)

Scientific name	English common name	Party Listing Species
FAUNA	**ANIMALS**	
MAMMALIA	***MAMMALS***	
Chiroptera		
Phyllostomidae		
Vampyrops lineatus	White-lined bat	UY
Edentata		
Myrmecophagidae		
Tamandua tetradactyla (=*Tamandua mexicana*)	Collared anteater	GT
Choloepidae		
Choloepus hoffmanni	Hoffman's two-toed sloth	CR
Dasypodidae		
Cabassous centralis	Northern naked-tailed armadillo	CR
C. tatouay (=*C.gymmurus*)	Greater naked-tailed armadillo	UY
Pholidotaa		
Manidae		
Manis gigantea	Giant pangolin	GH

Scientific name	English common name	Party Listing Species
M. tetradactyla (=M.longicauda)	Long-tailed pangolin	GH
M. tricuspis	Tree pangolin	GH

Rodentai

Sciuridae
Epixerus ebii	Temminck's giant squirrel	GH
Marmota caudata		IN
M. himalayana		IN
Sciurus deppei	Deppe's squirrel	CR

Anomaluridae
Anomalurus beecrofti	Beecroft's flying squirrel	GH
A. derbianus	Lord Derby's flying squirrel	GH
A. peli	Pel's flying squirrel	GH
Idiurus macrotis	Long-eared flying squirrel	GH

Hystricidae
Hystrix cristata	North African crested porcupine	GH

Erethizontidae
Sphiggurus mexicanus (=Coendou)	Mexican tree porcupine	HN
S. spinosus(=Coendou)	Spiny tree porcupine	UY

Agoutidae
Agouti paca(=Cuniculus)	Spotted paca	HN

Dasyproctidae
Dasyprocta punctata	Central American agouti	HN

Carnivora

Canidae
Canis aureus	Golden jackal	IN
Vulpes bengalensis	Bengal fox	IN
V. vulpes griffithi		IN
V. v. montana	Montana red fox	IN
V. v. pusilla (=leucopus)		IN

Scientific name	English common name	Party Listing Species
Procyonidae		
Bassaricyon gabbii	Bushy-tailed olingo	CR
Bassariscus sumichrasti	Central American cacomistle	CR
Nasua nasua (=*N. narica*)	Coati	HN
N. n. solitaria	South Brazilian coati	UY
Potos flavus	Kinkajou	HN
Mustelidae		
Eira barbara	Tayra	HN
Galictis vittata	Greater grison	CR
(=*G. allamandi*)		
Martes flavigula	Yellow-throated marten	IN
(=*M. gwatkinsi*)		
M. foina intermedia	Beech marten	IN
Mellivora capensis	Ratel	GH, BW
Mustela altaica	Mountain weasel	IN
M. erminea	Ermine	IN
M. kathiah	Yellow-bellied weasel	IN
M. sibirica	Siberian weasel	IN
Viverridae		
Arctitis binturong	Binturong	IN
Civettictis civetta	African civit	BW
(=*Viverra*)		
Paguma larvata	Masked palm civet	IN
Paradoxurus hermaphroditus	Palm civet	IN
P. jerdoni	Palm civet	IN
Viverra megaspila	Oriental civet	IN
V. zibetha	Oriental civet	IN
V. indica	Lesser oriental civet	IN
Herpestidae		
Herpestes auropunctatus	Small Indian mongoose	IN
H. edwardsi	Indian grey mongoose	IN
H. fuscus	Indian brown mongoose	IN
H. smithii	Ruddy mongoose	IN
H. urva	Crab-eating mongoose	IN

Scientific name	English common name	Party Listing Species
H. vitticollis	Stripe-necked mongoose	IN

Protelidae
| *Proteles cristatus* | Aardwolf | BW |

Pinnipedia

Odobenidae
| *Odobenus rosmarus* | Walrus | CA |

Artiodactyla

Hyppopotamidae
| *Hippopotamus amphibius* | Hippopotamus | GH |

Tragulidae
| *Hyemoschus aquaticus* | Water chevrotain | GH |

Cervidae
Cervus elaphus barbarus	Barbary red deer	TN
Mazama americana cerasina	Guatemalan red brocket	GT
Odocoileus virginianus mayensis	Guatemalan white-tailed deer	GT

Bovidae
Antilope cervicapra	Blackbuck	NP
Boocercus eurycerus (=*Tragelaphus eurycerus*)	Bongo	GH
Bubalus arnee (=*Bubalus bubalis*)	Water buffalo	NP
Damaliscus lunatus	Tsessebi	GH
Gazella cuvieri	Edmi gazelle	TN
G. dorcas	Dorcas gazelle	TN
G. leptoceros	Sand gazelle	TN
Tetracerus quadricornis	Four-horned antelope	NP
Tragelaphus spekei	Sitatunga	GH

Scientific name	English common name	Party Listing Species

AVES BIRDS

Ciconiformes

Ardeidae

Ardea goliath	Goliath heron	GH
Bubulcus ibis (*=Ardeola ibis*)	Cattle egret	GH
Casmerodius albus(*=Egretta alba*)	Great egret	GH
Egretta garzetta	Little egret	GH

Ciconiidae

Ephippiorhynchus senegalensis	Saddlebill stork	GH
Leptoptilos crumeniferus	Marabou stork	GH

Threskiornithidae

Hagedashia hagedash (*=Bostrychia hagedash*)	Hadada ibis	GH
Lampribis rara (*=Bostrychia rara*)	Spot-breasted ibis	GH
Threskiornis aethiopicus	Sacred ibis	GH

Anseriformes

Anatidae

Alopochen aegyptiacus	Egyptian goose	GH
Anas acuta	Northern pintail	GH
A. capensis	Cape teal	GH
A. clypeata (*=Spatula clypeata*)	Northern shoveler	GH
A. crecca	Common teal	GH
A. penelope	Eurasion wigeon	GH
A. querquedula	Garganey	GH
Aythya nyroca (*=Nyroca nyroca*)	Ferruginous duck	GH
Cairina moschata	Muscovy duck	HN
Dendrocygna autumnalis (*=Dendrocygna fulva*)	Black-bellied whistling duck	HN
D. bicolor (*=Dendrocygna fulva*)	Fulvous whistling duck	GH, HN
D. viduata	White-faced whistling duck	GH

Nettapus auritus	African pygmy goose	GH
Plectropterus gambensis	Spur-winged goose	GH
Pteronetta hartlaubii	Hartlaub's duck	GH
(=*Cairina hartlaubii*)		

Falconiformes

Cathartidae
| Sarcoramphus papa | King vulture | HN |

Galliformes

Cracidae
Crax alberti	Blue-billed curassow	CO
C. daubentoni	Yellow-knobbed curassow	CO
C. globulosa	Wattled curassow	CO
C. rubra	Great curassow	CO, CR, GT, HN
Ortalis vetula	Plain chachalaca	GT, HN
Pauxi pauxi (=*C.* pauxi)	Helmeted curassow	CO
Penelope purpurascens	Crested guan	HN
Penelopina nigra	Highland guan	GT

Phasianidae
Agelastes meleagrides	White-breasted guineafowl	GH
Agriocharis ocellata	Ocellated turkey	GT
A. charltonii	Chestnut-necklaced partridge	MY
Arborophila orientalis	Bar-backed partridge	MY
(=*Arborophila brunneopectus*)		
Caloperdix oculea	Ferruginous wood-partridge	MY
Lophura erythrophthalma	Crestless fireback pheasant	MY
L. ignita	Crested fireback pheasant	MY
Melanoperdix nigra	Black wood-partridge	MY
Polyplectron inopinatum	Mountain peacock-pheasant	MY
Rhizothera longirostris	Long-billed partridge	MY
Rollulus rouloul	Crested wood partridge	MY
Tragopan satyra	Satyr tragopan	NP

Charadriformes

Scientific name	English common name	Party Listing Species
Burhinidae		
Burhinus bistriatus	Double-striped thick-knee	GT

Columbiformes

Columbidae		
Columba guinea	Speckled pigeon	GH
C. iriditorques	Western bronze-naped pigeon	GH
(=*Turturoena iriditorques*)		
C. livia	Rock pigeon	GH
C. mayeri (=*Nesoenas mayeri*)	Pink pigeon	MU
C. unicincta	Afep pigeon	GH
Oena capensis	Namaqua dove	GH
Streptopelia decipiens	Mourning collared dove	GH
S. roseogrisea	African collared dove	GH
S. semitorquata	Red-eyed dove	GH
S. senegalensis	Laughing dove	GH
S. turtur	Western turtle dove	GH
S. vinacea	Vinaceous dove	GH
Treron calva (=*Treron australis*)	African green pigeon	GH
T. waalia	Bruce's green pigeon	GH
Turtur abyssinicus	Black-billed wood dove	GH
T. afer	Blue-spotted wood dove	GH
T. brehmeri(=*Calopelia brehmeri*)	Blue-headed wood dove	GH
T. tympanistria (=*Tympanistria tympanistria*)	Tambourine dove	GH

Psittsciformes

Psittacidae		
Psittacula krameri	Rose-ringed parakeet	GH

Cuculiformes

Musophagidae

Scientific name	English common name	Party Listing Species
Corythaeola cristata	Great blue turaco	GH
Crinifer piscator	Western grey plantain-eater	GH
Musophaga violacea	Violet turaco	GH
Tauraco macrorhynchus	Crested turaco	GH

Piciformes

Capitonidae
Semnornis ramphastinus		CO

Ramphastidae
Baillonius bailloni		AR
Pteroglossus castanotis		AR
Ramphastos dicolorus		AR
R. toco		AR
Selenidera maculirostris		AR

Passeriformes

Cotingidae
Cephalopterus ornatus	Amazonian umbrellabird	CO
C. penduliger	Long-wattled umbrellabird	CO

Muscicapidae
Bebrornis rodericanus	Rodrigues warbler	MU
Terpsiphone bourbonnensis (=Tchitrea bourbonnensis)	Mascarene paradise flycatcher	MU

Icteridae
Agelaius flavus (=Xanthopsar flavus)	Saffron-cowled blackbird	UY

Fringillidae
Serinus canicapillus (=Serinus gularis)	Black-faced canary	GH
S. leucopygius	White-rumped canary	GH
S. mozambicus	Yellow-fronted canary	GH

Scientific name	English common name	Party Listing Species
Estrildidae		
Amadina fasciata	Cut-throat	GH
Amandava subflava (=*Estrilda subflava*)	Orange-breasted waxbill	GH
Estrilda astrild	Common waxbill	GH
E. caerulescens	Lavender waxbill	GH
E. melpoda	Orange-cheeked waxbill	GH
E. troglodytes	Black-rumped waxbill	GH
L. rara	Black-bellied firefinch	GH
L. rubricata	Brown-backed firefinch	GH
L. rufopicta	Bar-breasted firefinch	GH
L. senegala	Red-billed firefinch	GH
L. vinacea (=*Lagonosticta larvata*)	Black-faced firefinch	GH
Lonchura bicolor (=*Spermestes*)	Black-breasted mannikin	GH
L. cantans (=*L. malabarica*)	Silverbill	GH
L. cucullata (=*Spermestes*)	Bronze mannikin	GH
L. fringilloides (=*Spermestes*)	Magpie mannikin	GH
Mandingoa nitidula (=*Hypargos nitidulus*)	Green-backed twinspot	GH
Nesocharis capistrata	White-cheeked oliveback	GH
Nigrita bicolor	Chestnut-breasted negro-finch	GH
N. canicapilla	Grey-crowned negro-finch	GH
N. fusconota	White-breasted negro-finch	GH
N. luteifrons	Pale-fronted negro-finch	GH
Ortygospiza atricollis	Common quail-finch	GH
Parmoptila rubrifrons (=*Parmoptila woodhousei*)	Antpecker	GH
Pholidornis rushiae	Tiny tit	GH
Pyrenestes ostrinus (=*Pyrenestes frommi*)	Black-bellied seedcracker	GH
Pytilia hypogrammica	Red-faced pytilia	GH
P. phoenicoptera	Red-winged pytilia	GH
Spermophaga haematina	Western bluebill	GH

Scientific name	English common name	Party Listing Species
Uraeginthus bengalus (=*Estrilda bengala*)	Red-cheeked cordon-bleu	GH

Ploceidae

Scientific name	English common name	Party Listing Species
Amblyospiza albifrons	Thick-billed weaver	GH
Anaplectes rubriceps (=*Anomalospiza imberbis*)	Cuckoo weaver	GH
Bubalornis albirostris	Black buffalo-weaver	GH
Euplectes afer	Yellow-crowned bishop	GH
E. ardens (=*Coliuspasser ardens*)	Red-collared widowbird	GH
E. franciscanus (=*E. orix*)	Red bishop	GH
E. hordeaceus	Red-crowned bishop	GH
E. macrourus (=*Caliuspasser macrourus*)	Yellow-shouldered widowbird	GH
Malimbus cassini	Black-throated malimbe	GH
M. malimbicus	Crested malimbe	GH
M. nitens	Blue-billed malimbe	GH
M. rubricollis	Red-necked malimbe	GH
M. scutatus	Red-vented malimbe	GH
Pachyphantes superciliosus (=*Ploceus superciliosus*)		GH
Passer griseus	Grey-headed sparrow	GH
Petronia dentata	Bush sparrow	GH
Plocepasser superciliosus	Chestnut-crowned sparrow-weaver	GH
Ploceus albinucha	White-naped weaver	GH
P. aurantius	Orange weaver	GH
P. cucullatus (=*Ploceus nigriceps*)	Village weaver	GH
P. heuglini	Heuglin's weaver	GH
P. luteolus (=*Sitagra luteola*)	Little weaver	GH
P. melanocephalus (=*Satigra malanocephala*)	Black-headed weaver	GH
P. nigerrimus	Black weaver	GH
P. nigricollis	Black-necked weaver	GH

P. pelzelni	Slender-billed weaver	GH
P. preussi	Golden-backed weaver	GH
P. tricolor	Yellow-mantled weaver	GH
P. vitellinus	Common masked weaver	GH
Quelea erythrops	Red-headed quelea	GH
Sporopipes frontalis	Speckle-fronted weaver	GH
Vidua chalybeata (=Hypochera chalybeata)	Village indigobird	GH
V. interjecta	Uelle paradise whydah	GH
V. larvaticola	Bako indigobird	GH
V. macroura	Pin-tailed whydah	GH
V. orientalis (=V. paradisaea)	Common paradise whydah	GH
V. raricola	Jambandu indigobird	GH
V. togoensis	Togo paradise whydah	GH
V. wilsoni	Wilson's lovebird	GH

Sturnidae

Gracula religiosa		TH

REPTILIA / REPTILES

Testudinata

Trionychidae

Trionyx triunguis	Nile soft-shell turtle	GH

Pelomedusidae

Pelomedusa subrufa	Helmeted turtle	GH
Pelusios adansoni	Adanson's mud turtle	GH
P. castaneus	West African mud turtle	GH
P. gabonensis (=Malimbus rubriceps)	African forest turtle	GH
P. niger	West African black forest turtle	GH

Serpentes

Colubridae

Atretium schistosum	Olive keelback watersnake	IN
Cerberus rhynchops	Dog-faced watersnake	IN
Xenochrophis piscator	Chequered keelback	IN

Scientific name	English common name	Party Listing Species
(=*Natrix* spp.)	watersnake	

Elapidae

Micrurus diastema	Atlantic coral snake	HN
M. nigrocinctus	Black-banded coral snake	HN

Viperidae

Agkistrodon bilineatus	Cantil	HN
Bothrops asper	Barba amarilla	HN
B. nasutus	Horned hog-nosed pit viper	HN
B. nummifer	Jumping viper	HN
B. ophryomegas		HN
B. schlegelii	Horned palm viper	HN
Crotalus durissus	Tropical rattlesnake	HN
Vipera russellii	Russell's viper	IN

FLORA   PLANTS

Gnetaceae
Gnetum montanum   NP

Magnoliaceae
Talauma hodgsonii   NP

Papaveraceae
Meconopsis regia   NP

Podocaraceae
Podocarpus neriifolius   NP

Tetracentraceae
Tetracentron sinense

Scientific name	*English common name*	*Party Listing Species*

*Coding guide for parties listing species:

AR— Argentina
BW— Botswana
CA— Canada
CO— Colombia
CN— China
CR— Costa Rica
GH— Ghana
GT— Guatemala
HN— Honduras
IN— India
MU— Mauritius
MY— Malaysia
NP— Nepal
TH— Thailand
TN— Tunisia
UY— Uruguay

Appendix B:
CITES Parties and Reservations

A s of April 1994, the following 122 countries are parties to the Convention on International Trade in Endangered Species of Wild Fauna and Flora (CITES).

PARTY	EFFECTIVE DATE
Afghanistan	28 January 1986
Algeria	21 Febuary 1984
Argentina	8 April 1981
Australia	27 October 1976
Austria	27 April 1982
Bahamas	18 September 1976
Bangladesh	18 February 1982
Barbados	9 March 1993
Belize	21 September 1981
Belgium	1 January 1984
Benin	28 May 1984
Bolivia	4 October 1979
Botswana	12 February 1978
Brazil	4 November 1975
Brunei Darussalem	2 August 1990
Bulgaria	16 April 1991
Burkina Faso	15 January 1990
Burundi	6 November 1988
Cameroon	3 September 1981
Canada	9 July 1975
Central African Rep.	25 November 1980
Chad	3 May 1989
Chile	1 July 1975
China, People's Rep.	8 April 1981
Colombia	29 November 1981

PARTY	EFFECTIVE DATE
Congo	1 May 1983
Costa Rica	28 September 1975
Cuba	19 July 1990
Cyprus	1 July 1975
Czech Republic	1 January 1993
Denmark	24 October 1977
Djibouti	7 May 1992
Dominican Republic	17 March 1987
Ecuador	1 July 1975
Egypt	4 April 1978
El Salvador	29 July 1987
Equatorial Guinea	8 June 1992
Estonia	20 October 1992
Ethiopia	4 July 1989
Finland	8 August 1976
France	9 August 1978
Gabon	15 May 1989
Gambia	24 November 1977
Germany	7 January 1976
Ghana	12 February 1976
Greece	6 January 1993
Guatemala	5 February 1980
Guinea	20 December 1981
Guinea-Bissau	16 May 1990
Guyana	25 August 1977
Honduras	13 June 1985
Hong Kong (see United Kingdom)	
Hungary	27 August 1985
India	18 October 1976
Indonesia	28 March 1979
Iran	1 November 1976
Israel	17 March 1980
Italy	31 December 1979
Japan	4 November 1980
Jordan	14 March 1979
Kenya	13 March 1979
Korea, Republic of	7 October 1993

PARTY	EFFECTIVE DATE
Liberia	9 June 1981
Liechtenstein	28 February 1980
Luxembourg	12 March 1984
Madagascar	18 November 1975
Malawi	6 May 1982
Malaysia	18 January 1978
Malta	16 July 1989
Mauritius	27 July 1975
Mexico	30 October 1991
Monaco	18 July 1978
Morocco	14 January 1976
Mozambique	23 June 1981
Namibia	18 March 1991
Nepal	16 September 1975
Netherlands	18 July 1984
New Zealand	8 August 1989
Nicaragua	4 November 1977
Niger	7 December 1975
Nigeria	1 July 1975
Norway	25 October 1976
Pakistan	19 July 1976
Panama	15 November 1978
Papua New Guinea	11 March 1976
Paraguay	13 February 1977
Peru	25 September 1975
Philippines	16 November 1981
Poland	12 March 1990
Portugal	11 March 1981
Russian Fed.	1 January 1992
Rwanda	18 January 1981
Saint Kitts and Nevis	15 May 1994
St. Lucia	15 March 1983
St. Vincent & Grenadines	28 February 1989
Senegal	3 November 1977
Seychelles	9 May 1977
Singapore	28 February 1987
Slovakia	1 January 1993
Somalia	2 March 1986

PARTY	EFFECTIVE DATE
South Africa	18 October 1975
Spain	28 August 1986
Sri Lanka	2 August 1979
Sudan	24 January 1983
Suriname	15 February 1981
Sweden	1 July 1975
Switzerland	1 July 1975
Tanzania	27 February 1980
Thailand	21 April 1984
Togo	21 January 1979
Trinidad & Tobago	18 April 1984
Tunisia	1 July 1975
Uganda	16 October 1991
United Kingdom (incl. Hong Kong	31 October 1976
United States	1 July 1975
United Arab Emirates	12 May 1990
Uruguay	1 July 1975
Vanuatu	15 October 1989
Venezuela	22 January 1978
Viet Nam	20 April 1994
Zaire	18 October 1976
Zambia	22 February 1981
Zimbabwe	17 August 1981

S PECIFIC RESERVATIONS ENTERED BY PARTIES (AS OF OCTOBER 7, 1993)

Appendix I

FAUNA

MAMMALIA

Cetacea

Physeteridae	*Physeter macrocephalus* =312	Japan, Norway
Ziphiidae	*Berardius* spp.	Russian Federation
	Berardius bairdii	Japan
	Hyperoodon spp.	Russian Federation
Balaenopteridae	*Balaenoptera acutorostrata* -101	Japan, Norway, Peru, Russian Federation
	Balaenoptera borealis (reservation not applicable to stocks(A) in North Pacific and (B) in area from 0 degrees longitude to 70 degrees east longitude, from the equator to theAntarctic Continent)	Japan, Norway
	Stocks (A) in North Pacific and (B) in area from 0 degrees longitude to 70 degrees east longitude, from the equator to the Antarctic Continent of *Balaenoptera borealis*	Russian Federation
	Balaenoptera edeni	Japan, Peru, Russian Federation
	Balaenoptera physalus	Japan
	Balaenoptera physalus (reservation not applicable to stocks (A) in	

123

North Atlantic off Iceland,
(B) in North Atlantic off
Newfoundland and (C) in area
from 40 degrees south latitude
to the Antarctic Continent,
from 120 degrees west longitude
to 60 degrees west longitude)   Russian Federation

Stocks (A) in North Atlantic
off Iceland, (B) in North Atlantic
off Newfoundland and (C) in
area from 40 degrees south latitude
to the Antarctic Continent, from
120 degrees west longitude to 60
degrees west longitude of
Balaenopter physalus   Norway
Megaptera novaeangliae   Saint Vincent and the
                                Grenadines

Balaenidae	*Caperea marginata*	Peru

Carnivora

Canidae	*Canis lupus* +202	Switzerland
Ursidae	*Ursus arctos isabellinus*	Switzerland
Mustelidae	*Lutra lutra*	Russian Federation
Felidae	*Acinonyx jubatus*	Namibia
	Felis caracal +205 =302	Switzerland
	Felis rubiginosa +206	Switzerland

Proboscidea

Elephantidae	*Loxodonta africana*	Botswana, Malawi, Namibia, South Africa, Zambia, Zimbabwe

Artiodactyla

Tayassuidae	*Catagonus wagneri*	Liechtenstein, Switzerland

Bovidae	*Pantholops hodgsoni*	Switzerland

AVES

Gruiformes

Otididae	*Chlamydotis undulata*	Switzerland

Columbiformes

Columbidae	*Caloenas nicobarica*	Switzerland

Psittaciformes

Psittacidae	*Ara macao*	Liechtenstein, Suriname, Switzerland

REPTILIA

Testudinata

Cheloniidae	*Chelonia mydas*	Cuba
	Chelonia mydas (reservation not applicable to the Australian population)	Suriname
	Eretmochelys imbricata	Cuba, Japan, Saint Vincent and the Grenadines
Dermochelyidae	*Dermochelys coriacea*	Suriname

Serpentes

Viperidae	*Vipera ursinii* +214	Liechtenstein, Switzerland

AMPHIBIA

Anura

Michrohylidae	*Dyscophus antongilii*	Liechtenstein, Switzerland

FLORA

Cactaceae

Disocactus spp. (reservation not applicable to *Discocactus horstii*)	Liechtenstein, Switzerland
Melocactus conoideus	Liechtenstein, Switzerland
Melocactus deinacanthus	Liechtenstein, Switzerland
Melocactus glaucescens	Liechtenstein, Switzerland
Melocactus paucispinus	Liechtenstein, Switzerland

Cupressaceae

Fitzroya cupressoides (reservation applicable only to the coastal population of Chile)	Chile

Orchidaceae

Renanthera imschootiana	Switzerland
Vanda coerulea	Switzerland

Appendix II

FAUNA

MAMMALIA

Carnivora

Canidae	*Canis lupus* -102	Russian Federation
Ursidae	*Ursidae* spp.	Republic of Korea (for 3 years)
Felidae	*Felis lynx*	Russian Federation

Artiodactyla

Cervidae	Moschus spp. -107	Republic of Korea (for 3 years)

AVES

Gruiformes

Pedionomidae	*Pedionomus torquatus*	Switzerland

Psittaciformes

Psittacidae	*Agapornis* spp.	Liechtenstein, Switzerland
	Amazona aestiva	Liechtenstein, Switzerland
	Amazona ochrocephala	Liechtenstein, Switzerland
	Aratinga spp.	Liechtenstein, Switzerland
	Cacatua galerita	Liechtenstein, Switzerland
	Cyanoliseus patagonus	Switzerland
	Cyanoliseus patagonus (reservation not applicable to C. p. byroni)	Liechtenstein
	Eoldophus roseicapillus	Liechtenstein, Switzerland
	Myiopsitta monachus	Liechtenstein, Switzerland
	Nandayus nenday	Liechtenstein, Switzerland
	Platycercus eximius	Liechtenstein, Switzerland
	Poicephalus senegalus	Liechtenstein, Switzerland
	Psittacula cyanocephala	Liechtenstein, Switzerland
	Pyrrhura spp.	Liechtenstein, Switzerland

Apodiformes

Trochilidae	*Trochilidae* spp.	Liechtenstein, Switzerland

REPTILIA

Sauria

Lacertidae	*Podarcis lilfordi*	Liechtenstein, Switzerland
	Podarcis pityusensis	Liechtenstein, Switzerland

AMPHIBIA

Anura

Dendrobatidae   *Dendrobates* spp.   Liechtenstein, Switzerland
                         Phyllobates spp.   Liechtenstein, Switzerland

PISCES

Cypriniformes

Cyprinidae   *Caecobarbus geertsi*   Liechtenstein, Switzerland

Appendix III

FAUNA

MAMMALIA

Carnivora

Canidae	*Canis aureus*	Liechtenstein, Switzerland
	Vulpes vulpes griffithi	France, Germany, Italy, Liechtenstein, Luxembourg, Netherlands, Portugal, Spain, Switzerland, United Kingdom
	Vulpes vulpes montana	France, Germany, Italy, Liechtenstein, Luxembourg, Netherlands, Portugal, Spain, Switzerland, United Kingdom
	Vulpes vulpes pusilla =402	France, Germany, Italy, Liechtenstein, Luxembourg, Netherlands, Portugal, Spain,

128

		Switzerland, United Kingdom
Mustelidae	*Martes foina intermedia*	Liechtenstein, Switzerland
	Mustela altaica	Liechtenstein, Switzerland
	Mustela erminea	France, Germany, Italy, Liechtenstein, Luxembourg, Netherlands, Portugal, Spain, Switzerland, United Kingdom
	Mustela kathiah	Liechtenstein, Switzerland
	Mustela sibirica	Liechtenstein, Switzerland

AVES

Psittaciformes

Psittacidae	*Psittacula krameri*	Liechtenstein, Switzerland

Interpretation

-101   Except: population of West Greenland

-102   Except: populations of Bhutan, India, Nepal and Pakistan

-107   Except: populations of Afghanistan, Bhutan, India, Myanmar, Nepal and Pakistan

+202   Populations of Bhutan, India, Nepal and Pakistan

+205   Population of Asia

+206   Population of India

+214   Population of Europe, except the area which formerly constituted the Union of Soviet Socialist Republics

=312   Includes synonym *Physeter catodon*

=322   Also referenced as *Lynx caracal*; includes generic synonym *Caracal*

=402   Includes synonym *Vulpes vulpes leucopus*

Appendix C:
List of Resolutions

EIGHTH MEETING OF THE CONFERENCE OF THE PARTIES TO CITES
KYOTO, JAPAN, MARCH 2–13, 1992

Resolutions:

Conf. 8.1
Financing and Budgeting of the Secretariat and of Meetings of the Conference of the Parties

Conf. 8.2
Implementation of the Convention in the European Economic Community (EEC)

Conf. 8.3
Recognition of the Benefits of Trade in Wildlife

Conf. 8.4
National Laws for Implementation of the Convention

Conf. 8.5
Standardization of CITES Permits and Certificates

Conf. 8.6
Role of the Scientific Authority

Conf. 8.7
Submission of Annual Reports

Conf. 8.8
Trade with States not Party to the Convention

Conf. 8.9
The Trade in Wild-Caught Animal Specimens

Conf. 8.10
Quotas for Leopard Hunting Trophies and Skins for Personal Use

Conf. 8.11
Stocks of Hair and Cloth of Vicuna

Conf. 8.12
Trade in Live Birds Experiencing High Mortalities in Transport

Conf. 8.13
Use of Coded-Microchip Implants for Marking Live Animals in Trade

Conf. 8.14
Universal Tagging System for the Identification of Crocodilian Skins

Conf. 8.15
Guidelines for a Procedure to Register and Monitor Operations Breeding
Appendix I Animal Species for Commercial Purposes

Conf. 8.16
Traveling Live Animal Exhibitions

Conf. 8.17
Improving the Regulation of Trade in Plants

Conf. 8.18
Standard References to the Names of Birds and Plants Listed in the Appendices

Conf. 8.19
Standard Reference to the Names of Orchidaceae

Conf. 8.20
Development of New Criteria for Amendment of the Appendices

Conf. 8.21
Consultation with Range States on Proposals to Amend Appendices I and II

Conf. 8.22
Additional Criteria for the Establishment of Captive Breeding Operations and for the Assessment of Ranching Proposals for Crocodilians

Conf. 8.23
Review of Appendix III

SEVENTH MEETING OF THE CONFERENCE OF THE PARTIES TO CITES
LAUSANNE, SWITZERLAND, OCTOBER 9–20, 1989

Resolutions:

Conf. 7.1
Membership of the Standing Committee

Conf. 7.2
Financing and Budgeting of the Secretariat and of Meetings of the Conference of the Parties

Conf. 7.3
Export/Re-export Permits/Certificates

Conf. 7.4
Control of Transit

Conf. 7.5
Enforcement

Conf. 7.6
Return of Live Animals of Appendix I or Appendix III Species

Conf. 7.7
Quotas for Leopard Hunting Trophies and Skins for Personal Use

Conf. 7.8
Trade in Ivory from African Elephants

Conf. 7.9
Terms of Reference for the Panel of Experts on the African Elephant and Criteria for the Transfer of Certain African Elephant Populations from

Appendix I to Appendix II

Conf. 7.10
Format and Criteria for Proposals to Register the First Commercial Captive Breeding Operation for an Appendix I Animal Species

Conf. 7.11
Trade in Ranched Specimens between Parties, Non-Parties and Reserving Parties

Conf. 7.12
Marking Requirements for Trade in Specimens of Taxa with Populations in Both Appendix I and Appendix II

Conf. 7.13
Shipment of Live Animals

Conf. 7.14
Special Criteria for the Transfer of Taxa from Appendix I to Appendix II

Conf. 7.15
Amendments to Appendix III

SIXTH MEETING OF THE CONFERENCE OF THE PARTIES TO CITES OTTAWA, CANADA, JULY 12–24, 1987

Resolutions:

Conf. 6.1
Establishment of Committee

Conf. 6.2
Financing and Budgeting of the Secretariat and of Meetings of the Conference of the Parties

Conf. 6.3
The Implementation of CITES

Conf. 6.4
Implementation of the Convention in Bolivia

Conf. 6.5
Implementation of CITES in the EEC

Conf. 6.6
Retrospective Issuance of Permits and Certificates

Conf. 6.7
Interpretation of Article XIV, Paragraph 1, of the Convention

Conf. 6.8
Implementation of the Convention with Regard to Personal and Household Effects

Conf. 6.9
Trade in Leopard Skins

Conf. 6.10
Trade in Rhinoceros Products

Conf. 6.11
Trade in African Elephant Ivory

Conf. 6.12
Integration of the Management of the African Elephant Ivory Trade Controls

Conf. 6.13
Improving, Coordinating and Financing African Elephant Ivory Trade Controls

Conf. 6.14
Registration of Raw Ivory Importers and Exporters

Conf. 6.15
Marking of Raw Ivory Cut Pieces

Conf. 6.16
Trade in Worked Ivory from African Elephants

Conf. 6.17
Implementation of the Export Quotas for Nile and Saltwater Crocodile Skins

Conf. 6.18
Additional Considerations for Plant Parts and Derivatives

Conf. 6.19
Additional Considerations for Artificially Propagated Hybrids of Appendix I Plants

Conf. 6.20
Standard Nomenclature for Cactus Plants

Conf. 6.21
Control Procedures for Commercial Captive Breeding Operations

Conf. 6.22
Monitoring and Reporting Procedures for Ranching Operations

Conf. 6.23
Guidelines for Evaluating Marine Turtle Ranching Proposals

Conf. 6.24
Shipment of Live Animals

FIFTH MEETING OF THE CONFERENCE OF THE PARTIES TO CITES BUENOS AIRES, ARGENTINA, APRIL 22–MAY 3, 1985

Resolutions:

Conf. 5.1
Financing and Budgeting of the Secretariat and of Meetings of the Conference of the Parties

Conf. 5.2
Implementation of the Convention in Bolivia

Conf. 5.3
Significant Trade in Appendix II Species

Conf. 5.4
Periodic Reports

Conf. 5.5
Annual Reports of Parties Which Are Members of a Regional Trade Agreement

Conf. 5.6
Trade Monitoring

Conf. 5.7
Time Validity of Import Permits

Conf. 5.8
Certificates of Origin for Appendix II Specimens

Conf. 5.9
Control of Readily Recognizable Parts and Derivatives

Conf. 5.10
Definition of "Primarily Commercial Purposes"

Conf. 5.11
Definition of the Term "Pre-Convention Specimen"

Conf. 5.12
Trade in Ivory from African Elephants

Conf. 5.13
Trade in Leopard Skins

Conf. 5.14
Improving the Regulation of Trade in Plants

Conf. 5.15
Improving and Simplifying the Regulation of Trade in Artificially Propagated Plants

Conf. 5.16
Trade in Ranched Specimens

Conf. 5.17
Identification Manual

Conf. 5.18
Air Transport of Live Wild Animals

Conf. 5.19
Nomenclature Committee

Conf. 5.20
Guidelines for the Secretariat When Making Recommendations in Accordance with Article XV

Conf. 5.21
Special Criteria for the Transfer of Taxa from Appendix I to Appendix II

Conf. 5.22
Criteria for the Inclusion of Species in Appendix III

FOURTH MEETING OF THE CONFERENCE OF THE PARTIES TO CITES
GABORONE, BOTSWANA, APRIL 19–30, 1983

Resolutions:

Conf. 4.1
The Standing Committee of the Conference of the Parties

Conf. 4.2
Payment of Travel Expenses for Standing Committee Members

Conf. 4.3
Financing and Budgeting of the Secretariat and of Meetings of the Conference of the Parties

Conf. 4.4
Amendment to the Name of the Technical Expert Committee

Conf. 4.5
Appointment of Technical Regional Coordinators

Conf. 4.6
Submission of Draft Resolutions and Other Documents for Meetings of the Conference of the Parties

Conf. 4.7
Regulation of Trade in Appendix II Wildlife and Implementation of Article IV, Paragraph 3, of the Convention

Conf. 4.8
Treatment of Exports of Parts and Derivatives Without Permit from a Party to Another Which Deems Them Readily Recognizable

Conf. 4.9
Time Validity of Export Permits and Re-export Certificates

Conf. 4.10
Definition of "In Transit"

Conf. 4.11
Interpretation of "Pre-Convention Acquisition"

Conf. 4.12
Control of Tourist Souvenir Specimens

Conf. 4.13
Trade in Leopard Skins

Conf. 4.14
Trade in Worked Ivory

Conf. 4.15
Control of Captive Breeding Operations in Appendix I Species

Conf. 4.16
Artificially Propagated Plants in Appendix II

Conf. 4.17
Re-export of Confiscated Specimens

Conf. 4.18
Disposal and Return of Illegally Traded Appendix II Specimens

Conf. 4.19
Identification Manual

THIRD MEETING OF THE CONFERENCE OF THE PARTIES TO CITES NEW DELHI, INDIA, FEBRUARY 25–MARCH 8, 1981

Conf. 3.4
Technical Cooperation

Conf. 3.5
Technical Expert Committee

Conf. 3.6
Standardization of Permits and Certificates Issued by Parties

Conf. 3.7
Security Measures

Conf. 3.8
Acceptance of Comparable Documentation Issued by States Not Party to the Convention

Conf. 3.9
International Compliance Control

Conf. 3.10
Review and Harmonization of Annual Reports

Conf. 3.11
Trade in Rhinoceros Horn

Conf. 3.12
Trade in African Elephant Ivory

Conf. 3.13
Trade in Whale Products

Conf. 3.14
Disposal of Confiscated or Accumulated Specimens of Appendix II Species

Conf. 3.15
Ranching

Conf. 3.16
Implementation of the Guidelines on Transport of Live Specimens

Conf. 3.17
International Reporting System for Specimens Stressed During Transport

Conf. 3.18
Identification Manual

Conf. 3.19
Index of Species Mentioned in Legislation

Conf. 3.20
Ten-Year Review of the Appendices

Conf. 3.21
Reverse Listing Concept for Appendices

SECOND MEETING OF THE CONFERENCE OF THE PARTIES TO CITES SAN JOSE, COSTA RICA, MARCH 19–30, 1979

Resolutions:

Conf. 2.1
Financing of the Secretariat and of Meetings of the Conference of the Parties

Conf. 2.2
Establishment of the Standing Committee of the Conference of the Parties

Conf. 2.3
External Funding of Special Programmes

Conf. 2.4
Project Proposal to the United Nations Environment Programme for the Development of an Identification Manual

Conf. 2.5
Harmonization of Permit Forms and Procedures

Conf. 2.6
Trade in Appendix II and III Species

Conf. 2.20
The Use of the Subspecies as a Taxonomic Unit in the Appendices

Conf. 2.21
Species Thought to be Extinct

Conf. 2.22
Trade in Feral Species

Conf. 2.23
Special Criteria for the Deletion of Species and Other Taxa Included in Appendix I or II Without Application of the Berne Criteria for Addition

FIRST MEETING OF THE CONFERENCE OF THE PARTIES TO CITES BERNE, SWITZERLAND, NOVEMBER 2–6, 1976

Resolutions:

Conf. 1.1
Criteria for the Addition of Species and Other Taxa to Appendices I and II and for the Transfer of Species and Other Taxa from Appendix II to Appendix I

Conf. 1.2
Criteria for the Deletion of Species and Other Taxa from Appendices I and II

Conf. 1.3
Deletion of Species from Appendix I or II in Certain Circumstances

Conf. 1.4
Museum and Herbarium Inventories

Conf. 1.5
Recommendations Concerning the Interpretation and Implementation of Certain Provisions of the Convention

Conf. 1.6
Resolutions Adopted by the Plenary Sessions

Conf. 1.7
Special Working Session on Implementation Issues

Conf. 1.8
Secretariat of the Convention

Conf. 1.9
Ratification or Accession by Non-party States

Appendix D:
TRAFFIC Offices

TRAFFIC International
219c Huntingdon Road, Cambridge CB3 ODL, United Kingdom. Tel: 44-223-277427. Fax: 44-223-277237. Tlx: 817036 SCMU G.

TRAFFIC Europe-Regional Office
Chaussee de Waterloo 608, B-1060 Brussels, Belgium. Tel: 32-2-3470111. Fax: 32-2-3440511. Tlx: 23986 WWFBEL B.

TRAFFIC Europe-France Office
c/o WWF-France, 151 Boulevard de la Reine, F-78000, Versailles, France. Tel: 33-1-39 24 2424. Fax: 33-1-39 53 0446. Tlx: 699153 F SORIA.

TRAFFIC Europe-Germany Office
Umwelstiftung WWF-Deutschland, Hedderich str. 110, 60591 Frankfurt (M) 70, Germany. Tel: 49-69-6050030. Fax: 49-69-617221. Tlx: 505990217 wwfd.

TRAFFIC Europe-Italy Office
c/o WWF-Italia, Via Salaria 290, 00199 Rome, Italy. Tel: 39-6-841 1712. Fax: 396 8413137.

TRAFFIC Europe-Netherlands Office
Postbus 7, 3700 AA Zeist, The Netherlands. Tel: 31-3404-37333. Fax: 31-3404-12064. Tlx: 76122 WNF NL.

TRAFFIC East/Southern Africa-Regional Office
c/o Chief Game Warden, Department of National Parks and Wildlife, P.O. Box 30131, Lilongwe 3, Malawi. Tel: (265) 743645. Fax: (265) 743648.

TRAFFIC East/Southern Africa-South Africa Office
c/o Endangered Wildlife Trust, Private Bag X11, Parkview 2122, Johannesburg, South Africa. Tel: 27-11-486 1102. Fax: 27-11-486-1506.

TRAFFIC East/Southern Africa-Tanzania Office
c/o PAWM, Department of Wildlife, P.O. Box 63150, Dar es Salaam, Tanzania.
Tel: 255-51-25593. Fax: 255-51-29355.

TRAFFIC India
172-B, Lodi Estate, New Delhi-110003, India. Tel: 91-11-4611258/4627582.
Fax: 91-11-463-2727.

TRAFFIC Japan
WWF-Japan, 7th Fl., Nihonseimei Akabanebashi Bldg., 3-1-14 Shiba, Minato-
ku 105, Tokyo, Japan. Tel: 81-33-7691716. Fax: 81-33-7691304. Tlx: 2428231
WWFJPN J.

TRAFFIC Oceania
8-12 Bridge Street, 10th Floor, P.O. Box R594, Royal Exchange, Sydney
N.S.W. 2000, Australia. Tel: 61-2-2478133. Fax: 61-2-2474579. Tlx: 73303
LVSTA AA.

TRAFFIC South America-Regional Office
Carlos Roxlo 1496/301, 11200 Montevideo, Uruguay. Tel/Fax: 598-2-49 3384.
Tlx: 23702 P. BOOTH UY.

TRAFFIC South America-Argentina Office
Ayacucho 1477, Suite 9B, Buenos Aires, Argentina. Tel/Fax: 54-1-8114348.

TRAFFIC Southeast Asia
Locked Bag No. 911, Jin. Sultan PO, 46990 Petaling Jaya, Selangor, Malaysia.
Tel: 60-3 7913159. Fax: 60-3 7175405.

TRAFFIC Taipei
3F, No. 7 Lane 49, Shih Ta Road, Ta An District, P.O. Box 7-476, Taipei,
Taiwan. Tel: 886-2-362 9787. Fax: 886-2-362 9799.

TRAFFIC USA
c/o WWF-US, 1250 24th St. N.W., Washington, DC 20037, USA. Tel: 202-
293-4800. Fax: 202-775-8287. Tlx: 64505 PANDA. E-Mail: EcoNet
"wwftraffic."

Suggested Readings

B

OOKS AND REPORTS

Abbott, R. Tucker. *Shell Trade in Florida*. Washington, D.C.: World Wildlife Fund, 1980.

Allen, Catherine M., and K.A. Johnson. *1990 Psittacine Captive Breeding Survey*. Washington, D.C.: TRAFFIC USA/World Wildlife Fund, 1990.

Axelrod, Herbert R., W.E. Burgess, and C.W. Emmens. *Exotic Marine Fishes*. 1969. Reprint, Neptune, N.J.: T.F.H. Publications, Inc., 1979.

_____. *Exotic Tropical Fishes*. Neptune, N.J.: T.F.H. Publications, Inc., 1980.

Axelrod, Herbert R., and W. Vorderwinkler. *Encyclopedia of Tropical Fishes*. Neptune, N.J.: T.F.H. Publications, Inc., 1980.

Bates, Henry, and R. Busenbark. *Finches and Softbilled Birds*. Neptune, N.J.: T.F.H. Publications, Inc., 1970.

Bean, Michael J. *The Evolution of National Wildlife Law*. 1977. Reprint, New York: Praeger Publishers, 1983.

Beissinger, Steven R., and N.F. Snyder. *New World Parrots in Crisis: Solutions from Conservation Biology*. Washington, D.C.: Smithsonian Institution Press, 1992.

Bensky, Dan, and A. Gamble. *Chinese Herbal Medicine: Materia Medica*. Seattle: Eastland Press, 1986.

Benson, Lyman. *The Cacti of the United States and Canada.* Stanford, Calif.: Stanford University Press, 1982.

Boardman, Robert. *International Organization and the Conservation of Nature.* Bloomington, Ind.: Indiana University Press, 1981.

Bräutigam, Amie. *CITES: A Conservation Tool: A Guide to Amending the Appendices to the Convention on International Trade in Endangered Species of Wild Fauna and Flora.* Gland, Switzerland: IUCN, 1991.

Browning, John G. *Tarantulas.* Neptune, N.J.: T.F.H. Publications, Inc., 1989.

Burton, John A., and B. Pearson. *The Collins Guide to the Rare Mammals of the World.* Lexington, Mass.: Stephen Greene Press, 1987.

Burton, Maurice, and R. Burton. *Encyclopedia of Insects and Arachnids.* 1968. Reprint, London: Octopus Books, 1975.

Callister, Debra J. *Illegal Tropical Timber Trade: Asia-Pacific.* Cambridge, United Kingdom: TRAFFIC International, 1993.

Carr, Archie. *Handbook of Turtles: The Turtles of the United States, Canada, and Baja California.* Ithaca, N.Y.: Cornell University Press, 1952.

Central Intelligence Agency. *The World Factbook.* Washington, D.C.: U.S. Government Printing Office, published annually.

Chadwick, Douglas H. *The Fate of the Elephant.* San Francisco: Sierra Club Books, 1992.

Chandler, William J., Ed. *Audubon Wildlife Report, 1988-1989.* New York: National Audubon Society, 1988.

Chandler, William J., and L. Labate, Eds. *Audubon Wildlife Report, 1989-1990.* New York: National Audubon Society, 1989.

Cobb, Stephen, Ed. *The Ivory Trade and the Future of the African Elephants.* Vols. I and II. Lausanne, Switzerland: CITES Secretariat, 1989.

Collar, Nigel J., and S.N. Stuart. *Threatened Birds of Africa and Related Islands: The ICBP/IUCN Red Data Book, Part 1.* 3rd ed. Gland, Switzerland: IUCN/ICBP, 1984.

Collar, Nigel J., and P. Andrew. *Birds to Watch: The ICBP World Checklist of Threatened Birds*. ICBP Technical Publication No. 8. Washington, D.C.: Smithsonian Institution Press, 1988.

Collins, N. Mark, and M.G. Morris. *Threatened Swallowtail Butterflies of the World: The IUCN Red Data Book*. Gland, Switzerland: IUCN, 1985.

Corbet, G.B., and J.E. Hill. *A World List of Mammalian Species*. 3rd. ed. New York: Oxford University Press, 1991.

Davis, S.D., et al. *Plants in Danger: What Do We Know?* Cambridge, United Kingdom: Threatened Plants Unit, 1984.

_____. *1994 IUCN Red List of Threatened Animals*. Gland, Switzerland: IUCN.

Day, David. *The Doomsday Book of Animals: A Natural History of Vanished Species*. New York: Viking Press, 1981.

De Meulenaer, Thomas, and J. Gray. *The Control of Wildlife Trade in Greece*. Cambridge, United Kingdom: TRAFFIC International, 1992.

Di Silvestro, Roger. *The Endangered Kingdom: The Struggle to Save America's Wildlife*. New York: John Wiley & Sons, 1989.

Di Silvestro, Roger, and E.S. Eno, Eds. *Audubon Wildlife Report*. New York: National Audubon Society, 1985.

_____, Eds. *Audubon Wildlife Report*. New York: National Audubon Society, 1986.

_____, Eds. *Audubon Wildlife Report*. New York: National Audubon Society, 1987.

Dublin, Holly T., and H. Jachmann. *The Impact of the Ivory Ban on Illegal Hunting of Elephants in Six Range States in Africa*. Gland, Switzerland: World-Wide Fund for Nature, 1992.

Dunlap, Thomas R. *Saving America's Wildlife*. Princeton, N.J.: Princeton University Press, 1991.

Durrell, Lee. *State of the Ark: An Atlas of Conservation in Action.* Garden City, N.Y.: Doubleday & Company, Inc., 1986.

Ehrlich, Paul R., D.S. Dobkin, and D. Wheye. *Birds in Jeopardy: The Imperiled and Extinct Birds of the United States and Canada: Including Hawaii and Puerto Rico.* Stanford, Calif.: Stanford University Press, 1992.

Ehrlich, Paul R., and A.H. Ehrlich. *Extinction: The Causes and Consequences of the Disappearance of Species.* New York: Ballantine Books, 1985.

_____. *The Population Explosion.* New York: Simon & Schuster, 1990.

Eisenberg, John F. *Mammals of the Neotropics: The Northern Neotropics.* Chicago: University of Chicago Press, 1989.

Engnath, Bob. *The Scrimshaw Connection.* Pasadena, Calif.: House of Muzzle Loading, 1982.

Environmental Investigation Agency. *Under Fire: Elephants on the Front Line.* London: Environmental Investigation Agency, 1992.

Ernst, Carl H., and R.W. Barbour. *Turtles of the United States.* Lexington, Ky.: University of Kentucky Press, 1972.

Espinoza, Edgard O., and M.J. Mann. *Identification Guide for Ivory and Ivory Substitutes.* Washington, D.C.: World Wildlife Fund, 1990.

Farrand, John, Jr., Ed. *The Audubon Society Encyclopedia of Animal Life.* New York: Alfred A. Knopf, 1982.

Favre, David S. *International Trade in Endangered Species: A Guide to CITES.* Boston: Martinus Nijhoff Publishers, 1989.

_____. *Wildlife Law.* Detroit: Lupus Publications, 1991.

Fitter, Richard S.R. *Wildlife for Man: How and Why We Should Conserve Our Species.* London: Collins, 1986.

Fitzgerald, Sarah. *International Wildlife Trade: Whose Business Is It?* Washington, D.C.: World Wildlife Fund, 1989.

Forshaw, Joseph M. *Parrots of the World*. 3rd ed. London: Blandford Press, 1989.

Freiberg, Marcos A., and J.G. Walls. *The World of Venomous Animals*. Neptune, N.J.: T.F.H. Publications, Inc., 1984.

Frost, Darrel R., Ed. *Amphibian Species of the World*. Lawrence, Kan.: Association of Systematics Collections and Allen Press, 1985.

Fuller, Douglas O. *Medicine from the Wild: An Overview of the U.S. Native Medicinal Plant Trade and Its Conservation Implications*. Washington, D.C.: TRAFFIC USA/World Wildlife Fund, 1991.

Fuller, Douglas O., and S. Fitzgerald, Eds. *Conservation and Commerce of Cacti and Other Succulents*. Washington, D.C.: World Wildlife Fund, 1987.

Fuller, Kathryn, B. Swift, A. Jorgenson, and A. Bräutigam. *Latin American Wildlife Trade Laws* (Rev. Ed.). Washington, D.C.: World Wildlife Fund, 1985.

Gaski, Andrea. *Bluefin Tuna: An Examination of the International Trade with an Emphasis on the Japanese Market*. Cambridge, United Kingdom: TRAFFIC International, 1993.

Gaski, Andrea, and K.A. Johnson. *Prescription for Extinction: Endangered Species and Patented Oriental Medicines in Trade*. Washington, D.C.: TRAFFIC USA/World Wildlife Fund, 1994.

Gibson, Thomas, et al. *International Trade in Plants: Focus on U.S. Exports and Imports*. Washington, D.C.: TRAFFIC-USA, 1981.

Golden Press. *The Golden Guide* series. New York: Golden Press.

Goodson, Gar. *The Many-Splendored Fishes of Hawaii*. Stanford, Calif.: Stanford University Press, 1985.

_____. *Fishes of the Atlantic Coast*. Stanford, Calif.: Stanford University Press, 1985.

Greenberg, Idaz. *Guide to Corals and Fishes*. Miami: Seahawk Press, 1977.

Greenway, James C., Jr. *Extinct and Vanishing Birds of the World*. New York: Dover Publications, Inc., 1967.

Groombridge, Brian. *The IUCN Amphibia-Reptilia Red Data Book, Part 1: Testudines-Crocodylia-Rhynchocephalia*. Gland, Switzerland: IUCN, 1982.

_____. *World Checklist of Threatened Amphibians and Reptiles*. 5th ed. Cambridge, United Kingdom: World Conservation Monitoring Centre, 1993.

_____, Ed. *Global Biodiversity: Status of the Earth's Living Resources*. London: Chapman & Hall, 1992.

Grumbine, R. Edward. *Ghost Bears: Exploring the Biodiversity Crisis*. Washington, D.C.: Island Press, 1992.

Grzimek, Bernhard. *Grzimek's Animal Life Encyclopedia*. New York: Van Nostrand Reinhold Company, 1974.

Halliday, Tim. *Vanishing Birds: Their Natural History and Conservation*. New York: Holt, Rinehart, & Winston, 1978.

Halliday, Tim, and K. Adler, Eds. *The Encyclopedia of Reptiles and Amphibians*. New York: Facts on File Publications, 1986.

Harcourt, Caroline, and J. Thornback. *Lemurs of Madagascar and the Comoros: The IUCN Red Data Book*. Gland, Switzerland: IUCN, 1990.

Harriman, Sarah. *The Book of Ginseng*. New York: Jove Publications, 1977.

Hawkes, Alex D. *Encyclopaedia of Cultivated Orchids*. London: Faber & Faber Ltd., 1965.

Hemley, Ginette. "International Wildlife Trade." In *Audubon Wildlife Report, 1988-1989*. W. Chandler, Ed. New York: National Audubon Society, 1988.

Hemley, Ginette, and J. Thomsen. *The World Trade in Birds of Prey*. Washington, D.C.: World Wildlife Fund, forthcoming.

Hoage, R.J., Ed. *Animal Extinctions: What Everyone Should Know*. Washington, D.C.: Smithsonian Institution Press, 1985.

Howard, Richard, and A. Moore. *A Complete Checklist of the Birds of the World*. 2nd ed. Academic Press, 1991.

Huxley, Anthony. *Green Inheritance: The World Wildlife Fund Book of Plants.* Garden City, N.Y.: Doubleday, 1985.

Hykle, Douglas J. "An Evaluation of Canada's Implementation and Enforcement of CITES: The Convention on International Trade in Endangered Species of Wild Fauna and Flora." Master's thesis, Dalhousie University, Halifax, Nova Scotia, 1988.

Inskipp, Tim. *World Checklist of Threatened Mammals.* 2nd ed. Cambridge, United Kingdom: World Conservation Monitoring Centre, 1993.

Inskipp, Tim, and S. Wells. *International Trade in Wildlife.* London: International Institute for Environment and Development, 1979.

International Union for Conservation of Nature and Natural Resources (IUCN) Environmental Law Centre. *African Wildlife Laws.* Bonn, Germany: IUCN, 1986.

Jenkins, Martin, and S. Oldfield. *Wild Plants in Trade.* Cambridge, United Kingdom: TRAFFIC International, 1992.

Johnson, Kurt A. *1991 Psittacine Captive Breeding Survey.* Washington, D.C.: TRAFFIC USA/World Wildlife Fund, 1991.

King, Judith E. *Seals of the World.* Ithaca, N.Y.: Cornell University Press, 1991.

King, Stephen T., and J.R. Schrock *Controlled Wildlife. A Three-Volume Guide to U.S. Wildlife Laws and Permit Procedures.* Lawrence, Kan.: Association of Systematics Collections, 1985.

King, Warren B. *Endangered Birds of the World: The ICBP Bird Red Data Book.* Cambridge, United Kingdom: ICBP, 1981.

Klinowska, Margaret. *Dolphins, Porpoises, and Whales of the World: The IUCN Red Data Book.* Gland, Switzerland: IUCN, 1991.

Kohm, Kathryn A., Ed. *Balancing on the Brink of Extinction: The Endangered Species Act and Lessons for the Future.* Washington, D.C.: Island Press, 1991.

Koopowitz, Harold, and H. Kaye. *Plant Extinction: A Global Crisis.* Washington, D.C.: Stone Wall Press, 1983.

Leader-Williams, Nigel. *The World Trade in Rhino Horn: A Review*. Cambridge, United Kingdom: TRAFFIC International, 1992.

Lean, Geoffrey, D. Hinrichsen, and A. Markham. *Atlas of the Environment*. New York: Prentice Hall, 1990.

Lee, P.C., J. Thornback, and E.L. Bennett. *Threatened Primates of Africa: The IUCN Red Data Book*. Gland, Switzerland: IUCN, 1988.

Lewington, Anna. *Medicinal Plants and Plant Extracts: A Review of Their Importation into Europe*. Cambridge, United Kingdom: TRAFFIC International, 1993.

Littell, Richard. *Endangered and Other Protected Species: Federal Law and Regulation*. Washington, D.C.: Bureau of National Affairs, Inc, 1992.

Long, John L. *Introduced Birds of the World*. London: David & Charles, 1981.

Low, Rosemary. *Endangered Parrots*. Dorset, United Kingdom: Blandford Press, 1984.

Lyster, Simon. *International Wildlife Law*. Cambridge, United Kingdom: Grotius Publications Ltd., 1985.

Macdonald, David W., Ed. *The Encyclopedia of Mammals*. New York: Facts on File Publications, 1984.

Mack, David, and R.A. Mittermeier, Eds. *The International Primate Trade*. Vol. 1. Washington, D.C.: TRAFFIC USA/World Wildlife Fund, 1984.

Marshall, Nina T. *The Gardener's Guide to Plant Conservation*. Washington, D.C.: World Wildlife Fund, 1993.

Martin, Esmond B. *The Japanese Ivory Industry*. Tokyo: World Wildlife Fund-Japan, 1985.

Martin, Esmond B., and C.B. Martin. *Run Rhino Run*. London: Chatto & Windus, 1982.

Mattison, Chris. *Snakes of the World*. New York: Facts on File Publications, 1986.

_____. *Frogs and Toads of the World*. New York: Facts on File Publications, 1987.

Medem, Federico. *Crocodile Skin Trade in South America*. Washington, D.C.: TRAFFIC USA/World Wildlife Fund, 1985.

Mehrtens, J.M. *Living Snakes of the World in Color*. New York: Sterling Publishing Company, Inc., 1987.

Milliken, Tom, K. Nowell, and J.B. Thomsen. *The Decline of the Black Rhino in Zimbabwe: Implications for Future Rhino Conservation*. Cambridge, United Kingdom: TRAFFIC International, 1993.

Mills, Judy A., and C. Servheen. *The Asian Trade in Bears and Bear Parts*. Washington, D.C.: TRAFFIC USA/World Wildlife Fund, 1991.

Musgrave, Ruth S., and M.A. Stein. *State Wildlife Laws Handbook*. Rockville, Md.: Government Institutes, Inc., 1993.

Myers, Norman. *Sinking Ark: A New Look at the Problem of Disappearing Species*. New York: Pergamon Press, 1979.

Myers, Norman, Ed. *Gaia: An Atlas of Planet Management*. London: Pan Books, 1985.

Nash, Stephen V. *Sold for a Song: The Trade in Southeast Asian Non-CITES Birds*. Cambridge, United Kingdom: TRAFFIC International, 1994.

National Research Council. *Decline of the Sea Turtles: Causes and Prevention*. Washington, D.C.: National Academy Press, 1990.

National Wildlife Federation. *Conservation Directory*. Washington, D.C.: National Wildlife Federation, published annually.

Nichols, David G., Jr., K.S. Fuller, E. McShane-Caluzi, and E. Klerner-Eckenrode. *Wildlife Trade Laws of Asia and Oceania*. Washington, D.C.: World Wildlife Fund, 1991.

Nichols, John. *The Animal Smugglers*. New York: Facts on File, 1987.

Nilsson, Greta. *The Bird Business*. Washington, D.C.: Animal Welfare Institute, 1981.

_____. *The Endangered Species Handbook*. Washington, D.C.: Animal Welfare Institute, 1983.

Norse, Elliott A. *Global Marine Biological Diversity: A Strategy for Building Conservation into Decision Making*. Washington, D.C.: Island Press, 1993.

Norton, John. *World Checklist of Threatened Birds*. 3rd ed. Cambridge, United Kingdom: World Conservation Monitoring Centre, 1993.

Nowak, Ronald M. *Walker's Mammals of the World*. 5th ed. Baltimore: Johns Hopkins Press, 1991.

Nowell, Kristin, Chyi Wei Lien, and P. Chica-jai. *The Horns of a Dilemma: The Market for Rhino Horn in Taiwan*. Cambridge, United Kingdom: TRAFFIC International, 1992.

Ono, Dana R., et al. *Vanishing Fishes of North America*. Washington, D.C.: Stone Wall Press, 1983.

Parker, Ian S.C., and M. Amin. *Ivory Crisis*. London: Chatto & Windus, 1983.

Peterson, Sandy. *The Peterson Field Guide* series. New York: Houghton-Mifflin Company.

_____. *What's Wildlife Worth?: Economic Contributions of Wild Plants and Animals to Developing Countries*. London: International Institute for Environment and Development, 1982.

Prescott-Allen, Christine, and R. Prescott-Allen. *The First Resource: Wild Species in the North American Economy*. New Haven, Conn.: Yale University Press, 1986.

Pritchard, Peter C. *Encyclopedia of Turtles*. Neptune, N.J.: T.F.H. Publications, Inc., 1979.

Reisner, Marc. *Game Wars: The Undercover Pursuit of Wildlife Poachers*. New York: Penguin Books, 1991.

Robinson, John G., and K.H. Redford, Eds. *Neotropical Wildlife Use and Conservation.* Chicago: Chicago University Press, 1991.

Rose, Debra A. *A North American Free Trade Agreement: The Impacts on Wildlife Trade.* Washington, D.C.: TRAFFIC USA/World Wildlife Fund, 1991.

Schaller, George B. *The Last Panda.* Chicago: University of Chicago Press, 1993.

Sheeline, Lenora. *Cultural Significance of Pacific Fruit Bats (Pteropus) to the Chamorro People of Guam.* Washington, D.C.: TRAFFIC USA/World Wildlife Fund, 1993.

Simon & Schuster. *The Simon & Schuster Field Guide* series. New York: Simon & Schuster Co.

Slack, Adrian. *Carnivorous Plants.* Cambridge, Mass.: Massachusetts Institute of Technology Press, 1980.

Soule, Michael E., Ed. *Conservation Biology: The Science of Scarcity and Diversity.* Sunderland, Mass.: Sinauer Associates, 1986.

Subik, Rudolf. *Cacti and Succulents.* London: Hamlyn Publishers, Ltd., 1972.

Swanson, Timothy M., and E.B. Barbier, Eds. *Economics for the Wilds: Wildlife, Wildlands, Diversity, and Development.* Washington, D.C.: Island Press, 1992.

Temple, Stanley A., Ed. *Endangered Birds: Management Techniques for Preserving Threatened Species.* Madison, Wisc.: University of Wisconsin Press, 1977.

Thomsen, Jorgen B. *Recent U.S. Imports of Certain Products from the African Elephant.* Washington, D.C.: TRAFFIC USA/World Wildlife Fund, 1987.

Thomsen, Jorgen B., S.R. Edwards, and T.A. Mulliken. *Perceptions, Conservation and Management of Wild Birds in Trade.* Cambridge, United Kingdom: TRAFFIC International, 1992.

Thornback, Jane, and M. Jenkins. *The IUCN Mammal Red Data Book, Part 1.* Gland, Switzerland: IUCN, 1981.

Tobin, Richard. *The Expendable Future: U.S. Politics and the Protection of Biological Diversity*. Durham, N.C.: Duke University Press, 1990.

TRAFFIC International. *The Smuggling of Endangered Wildlife Across the Taiwan Strait*. Godalming, United Kingdom: TRAFFIC International, 1991.

Trexler, Mark C. "The Convention on International Trade in Endangered Species of Wild Fauna and Flora: Political or Conservation Success?" Doctoral thesis, University of California, Berkeley, 1990.

Trexler, Mark C., and L. Kosloff. *The Wildlife Trade and CITES: An Annotated Bibliography for the Convention on International Trade in Endangered Species of Wild Fauna and Flora*. Washington, D.C.: World Wildlife Fund, 1987.

Tropical Agriculture Training Center (CATIE). *Status and Trends in International Trade and Local Utilization of Wildlife in Central America*. Costa Rica: Tropical Agriculture Training Center, 1984.

Vevers, Gwyne. *The Simon & Schuster Pocket Guide to Aquarium Fishes*. New York: Simon & Schuster, 1985.

Vinter, F. Jean. *Facts About Furs*. Washington, D.C.: Animal Welfare Institute, 1981.

Wagner, Robert J.L., and R.T. Abbott. *Standard Catalog of Shells*. Greenville, Del.: American Malacologists, Inc., 1978.

Watson, Allan, and P.E.S. Whalley. *The Dictionary of Butterflies and Moths in Color*. New York: Exeter Books, 1975.

Weissgold, Bruce J. "Controlling International Commerce in Endangered Species: Strenghtening CITES in an Ambivalent Environment." Master's thesis, University of Virginia, 1991.

Wells, Susan M., R.M. Pyle, and N.M. Collins. *The IUCN Invertebrate Red Data Book: A Contribution to the Global Environment Monitoring System*. Gland, Switzerland: IUCN, 1983.

Whitlock, Ralph. *Birds at Risk: A Comprehensive World-Survey of Threatened Species*. Wiltshire, United Kingdom: Moonraker Press, 1981.

Wijnstekers, Willem. *The Evolution of CITES: A Reference Guide to the Convention on International Trade in Endangered Species of Wild Fauna and Flora.* 3rd ed. Lausanne, Switzerland: CITES Secretariat, 1992.

Williams, John G., and A.E. Williams. *Field Guide to Orchids of North America.* New York: Universe Books, 1983.

Wilson, Don E., and D.M. Reeder, Eds. *Mammal Species of the World: A Taxonomic and Geographic Reference.* 2nd Ed. Washington, D.C.: Smithsonian Institution Press, 1993.

Wilson, Edward O., Ed. *Biodiversity.* Washington, D.C.: National Academy Press, 1988.

_____. *The Diversity of Life.* New York: W.W. Norton & Co., 1992.

Wood, Elizabeth W. *Coral Reefs of the World.* Neptune, N.J.: T.F.H. Publications, Inc., 1983.

_____. *Exploitation of Coral Reef Fishes for the Aquarium Trade.* Ross-on-Wye, United Kingdom: Marine Conservation Society, 1985.

World Conservation Monitoring Centre. *Global Biodiversity: Status of the Earth's Living Resources.* London: Chapman & Hall, 1992.

PERIODICALS

Bioscience. Published monthly by the American Institute of Biological Sciences, Washington, D.C.

Conservation Biology. Published quarterly by the Society for Conservation Biology, Cambridge, Mass.

Conservation Issues. Published bimonthly by World Wildlife Fund, Washington, D.C.

Endangered Species Technical Bulletin. Published monthly by the U.S. Department of the Interior, Washington, D.C.

IUCN Bulletin. Published quarterly by the International Union for Conservation of Nature and Natural Resources, Gland, Switzerland.

Oryx. Published quarterly by the Flora and Fauna Preservation Society of London.

Species: Newsletter of the SSC. Published quarterly by the Species Survival Commission of the International Union for Conservation of Nature and Natural Resources (IUCN), Gland, Switzerland.

TRAFFIC Bulletin. Published quarterly by TRAFFIC International, Cambridge, United Kingdom.

TRAFFIC USA. Published periodically by World Wildlife Fund, Washington, D.C.

Index